EZ series™

Writing Effective
E-MAIL

Practical Strategies for Strengthening
Electronic Communication

Verne Meyer

Pat Sebranek

John Van Rys

UPWRITE  PRESS®
We Make Writing Work For You. ®

Acknowledgements

Editorial Director: Patrick Sebranek
Director of Marketing: Thomas Spicuzza
Cover Design: Colleen Belmont, Chris Krenzke
Illustrations: Chris Krenzke
Editorial: Mariellen Hanrahan, Mary Anne Hoff, Rob King, Joyce Becker Lee,
    Ellen Leitheusser, Barb Lund, Verne Meyer, Kevin Orfield, Janae Sebranek,
    Lester Smith, John Van Rys, Claire Ziffer
Design and Production: Colleen Belmont, Tammy Hintz, Kevin Nelson,
    Christine Rieker, Kathy Strom

2 3 4 5 6 7 8 9 10 -FRZ- 11 10 09 08 07 06
ISBN 978-1-932436-03-7
ISBN 1-932436-03-0
Printed in Canada

Writing Effective E-Mail

Writing Effective E-Mail makes it possible for business workers to participate in worldwide communications quickly and easily. The digital era makes communication skills quite different from those used in past decades. That is why employers—and employees—are so interested in developing skills and strategies that make e-mail messages clear and effective.

Writing Effective E-Mail makes it possible for anyone to easily learn proven strategies and to write effective e-mails with the following traits:

- strong, clear ideas and specific details;
- an organization that helps make the content easy to follow;
- a voice that sounds sincere and knowledgeable;
- precise words that help build understanding;
- carefully written sentences that hold a reader's interest;
- correct capitalization, punctuation, and spelling; and
- a design that makes the message clear and appealing.

Bonus!

The writing activities and exercises included in *Writing Effective E-Mail* help users practice the skills they need to deliver effective messages. Reference pages give writers information to use in a variety of writing situations.

Table of Contents

Section 3: Models and Activities

Section 1
Management Policies

in this section

E-Mail Practices and Policies

Some people don't give much thought to e-mail. After all, how hard is it to dash off a message and press "Send"? But that's the problem. The simplicity of e-mail can make it an incredible asset in the business world—or a tremendous liability.

Therefore, companies need effective strategies for handling e-mail. This chapter offers guidelines for developing sound e-mail practices and policies. As you'll soon see, there's more to e-mail than simply sending a letter over electrical lines.

Your Goal

Understand what practices make up an e-mail policy.

3 Keys to Understanding E-Mail Policy

1 Employees should follow sound e-mail practices.

2 Employers should establish clear e-mail policies.

3 Disclaimer statements can provide added protection.

Follow Sound E-Mail Practices

E-mail communication is essential to business. Well-written messages convey a professional image, improve efficiency, and protect against liability. Badly written messages can be embarrassing, confusing, and even legally disastrous. To avoid such problems, all employees who send and receive e-mail messages should follow these 10 practices of business e-mail . . .

10 Practices

1. Imagine Your Message on a Billboard. Too often, a confusing, error-filled message gets sent to everyone in a company, and then to people outside. Employees should not send e-mail that they don't want to become public.

2. Remember That Company E-Mails Are Company Property. Because all e-mail sent from a company computer is technically company property, these messages may be monitored and examined by people other than the sender and receiver.

3. Avoid Offensive Comments. Libelous, defamatory, offensive, racist, or obscene comments do not belong in company e-mails—even as jokes.

4. Read Every Message Before Sending It. After completing a message, the sender should read the material to check for clarity and errors. Most embarrassing errors can be caught in this way.

5. Think Before Sending Confidential Information. Because e-mails may be read by people other than the recipient, e-mail messages should not be used to share unencrypted, confidential information.

# of Business E-Mail

6. <u>Avoid Emoticons and Initialisms.</u> Though common in personal e-mail messages, emoticons and initialisms are not professional and may cause confusion in business messages.

7. <u>Keep the Message "Cool."</u> Strong emotion can often be misread in e-mail messages. Business e-mails should not use multiple exclamation points, words in all capital letters, inflammatory phrases, or other overly emotional language.

8. <u>Think Carefully Before Forwarding Messages.</u> If the original sender had wanted the message sent to another person, he or she would have done so. When in doubt, it is best to get the sender's permission.

9. <u>Include the Message Thread.</u> Set your e-mail preferences to include the original message with the response. Doing so each time messages go back and forth keeps a helpful record of the digital "conversation."

10. <u>Reply Responsibly.</u> People generally expect a quick response to their e-mail messages. The recipient should try to reply to messages within 24 hours—ideally within the same working day. Also, when replying, the writer should make sure to answer every question asked in the previous message, thus avoiding unnecessary follow-ups.

Establish an E-Mail Policy

In addition to the general practices listed on pages 4 and 5, each company should create its own specific e-mail policy. A policy that spells out the rules governing e-mail use limits a company's exposure to liability and demonstrates that the company has made reasonable efforts to prevent inappropriate use. The components of an e-mail policy appear below, with a sample policy on page 7.

Appropriate use indicates what business e-mail may be used for.

Confidential data gives the policy for using e-mail to send sensitive information.

Inappropriate use indicates what business e-mail may not be used for.

Personal use tells whether business e-mail may be used for private matters.

Limit of privacy informs employees about their privacy rights regarding company e-mail messages.

Disclaimer indicates any disclaimers to be used with company e-mails.

Memo

Date: May 3, 2005
To: All Employees
From: Bill Frisk
Subject: New Centaur Press E-Mail Policy

Please sign and date the following e-mail policy, make a copy of it, and return the original to Bill Frisk in Information Technology.

- **Appropriate use:** E-mail may be used for most internal company correspondence, including memos, project updates, and meeting agendas. E-mail also may be used for external communications that are not confidential.

- **Confidential data:** When confidential data must be sent within the company, the e-mail must be encrypted. Confidential data—such as trade secrets, details about acquisitions, and so forth—should not be sent outside the company using e-mail.

- **Inappropriate use:** Centaur Press e-mail cannot be used to create or distribute content that is libelous, offensive, defamatory, obscene, threatening, or discriminatory.

- **Personal use:** Centaur Press e-mail can be used for personal use on a limited basis. As a rule, any given employee should send or receive no more than two or three personal messages per day.

- **Limit of privacy:** All e-mails created using Centaur Press computers are considered company property and thus are legally subject to monitoring. Also, all e-mail messages are stored on the server for up to seven years.

- **Disclaimer:** All e-mail messages sent outside the company must carry the virus disclaimer, which follows:

  Centaur Press has taken reasonable precautions to ensure this message does not contain a computer virus. Centaur Press accepts no liability for damage caused by a virus transmitted by this e-mail.

I have read and will abide by the Centaur Press e-mail policy.

_____   _____

(signature)   (date)

Use Disclaimer Statements

There are at least five reasons why your company may wish to add disclaimers to e-mails.

1. **Employer liability.** Companies are ultimately responsible for the actions of their employees. A disclaimer, however, can help reduce exposure to liability.

   Example: *Views and opinions expressed in this e-mail message are those of the author and do not represent the views of this company.*

   Example: *Company policy prohibits employees from making defamatory statements. This company accepts no liability for any such statements, and the employee will be held personally liable for any damages.*

2. **Confidentiality.** If an e-mail includes confidential information, a disclaimer can be used to legally bind the reader to confidentiality.

   Example: *This e-mail message includes confidential information and is intended solely for the person to whom it is addressed. If you are not the intended recipient and have received this message in error, please notify the sender immediately and delete this message from your system. Disclosing, disseminating, copying, or distributing this information is strictly prohibited.*

FYI

Note that disclaimers cannot fully protect a company against liability, but they can reduce its responsibility. Disclaimers demonstrate that a company is doing all it can to prevent any misuse—by employees or others—of the e-mails sent from the company. Disclaimers are also good reminders to employees to follow company policy.

3. **Contracts.** To prevent certain employees from unintentionally entering into agreements, include a disclaimer that the message does not constitute a contract.

> **Example:** *This e-mail message does not constitute a binding agreement on behalf of [COMPANY NAME].*

4. **Viruses.** A disclaimer such as the one below can help protect the company if an employee sends a message containing a virus to another company.

> **Example:** *This company has taken reasonable precautions to ensure this message does not contain a computer virus. This company does not accept liability for damage caused by a virus transmitted by this e-mail. As a further precaution, we recommend that the recipient check any attachments for the presence of computer viruses.*

5. **Contact Liability.** By law, your company is legally responsible for actions taken based on advice given to a third party if the advice is reasonably relied upon. This includes professional advice given by an employee in an e-mail message. A disclaimer can help protect against this kind of liability.

> **Example:** *[COMPANY NAME] is not liable for the consequences of any actions taken based on the content of this message unless an agreement is confirmed in writing.*

Implement the Policy

Give every employee a copy of your e-mail policy and make it available on the company intranet. (You may also want to attach the list of sound e-mail practices found on pages 4 and 5.) Train new employees on the policy and the need for strict compliance. Have employees sign and date a copy to add to their personnel file.

If the Company Monitors E-Mail . . .

Your policy should state that any use of e-mail (such as those listed below) that violates company policy is subject to discipline, up to and including termination.

- **HARASSMENT:** Forbid employees from using e-mail to hound colleagues or clients. A large number of messages may provide the basis for a harassment claim, so your policy should address frequency and number of e-mails.

- **FLAMING:** Forbid flaming and include a precise definition in your policy (for example, *language that is deliberately insulting, abusive, derogatory, threatening, or humiliating*).

Sound Advice

Have procedures in place to deal with complaints. If an incident occurs, deal with it fairly, quickly, and professionally.

Checklist for Developing an E-Mail Policy

Use the following components when you develop a company e-mail policy. (See pages 4-7.)

_____ **Appropriate use**

_____ **Confidential data**

_____ **Inappropriate use**

_____ **Personal use**

_____ **Limit of privacy**

_____ **Disclaimers**

_____ **Sound e-mail practices**

2

Manage Via **E-Mail**

Your business is modern, so your communication system should be as well. The era of telecommuting and remote work teams demands fast, efficient communications between managers and employees. E-mail can provide that link. With its ability to reach across organizational and geographic boundaries, e-mail has transformed business. This chapter will help you unlock the power of e-mail as a management tool.

Your **Goal**

● Write e-mails that help you build and manage a team.

4 Keys to Manage Via E-Mail

1 Use e-mail to build a team.

2 Use e-mail to develop a project.

3 Use e-mail to show personal interest.

4 Use the "Do's and Don'ts" of e-mail managing.

E-Mail as a Management Tool

E-mail is well suited to a variety of management tasks, such as assigning work, setting expectations, and monitoring progress. In addition to performing these tasks, e-mail can be used to build networks and create cooperation.

Build a Team

E-mail can help build teams, especially those with remote members. It can also allow team members to brainstorm—bounce ideas off one another—even when members are in different buildings, states, or countries.

Send out regular team updates. Include specifics, such as project names and dates and performance figures.

Foster team spirit by providing positive feedback and celebrating team success.

New Message

To: (Customer Retention Team)

Cc:

Subject: Thanks for a Great Year!

Dear Team:

One year ago today, the Customer Retention Team met for the first time. Since then, customer retention has increased 20 percent in a single year, which far exceeds our industry's average. That's an amazing achievement. I appreciate the long hours and hard work you have all contributed to this important project.

Thanks for your dedication!

Rick Reynolds

Develop a Project

E-mail can ease the development stage of a project. E-mail messages provide a rapid way to share and document information, discussions, and decisions.

Ask for suggestions within a certain time frame. Gather the suggestions and synthesize them into a project proposal.

⦿ ⦿ ⦿	New Message ⬭
To:	Carl Sanders, Suzanne Krenze, Devoy Johnson
Cc:	Linda Reynolds
Subject:	Dubuque Metalworks Partnering Ideas

Dear Team:

As you know, Dubuque Metalworks has indicated an interest in partnering with LNM Manufacturing. We're interested in pursuing this relationship, but we need to brainstorm a few business models before our meeting with them Tuesday. Please take a moment today to reply to this e-mail with any ideas you have.

Ellen Tuttle

Follow up with additional information, and ask for team input on the developing project.

⦿ ⦿ ⦿	New Message ⬭
To:	Carl Sanders, Suzanne Krenze, Devoy Johnson
Cc:	Linda Reynolds
Subject:	Dubuque Metalworks Partnering Proposal

Dear Team:

Thanks for the great input on the Dubuque Metalworks partnership. I have incorporated all your ideas in a proposal for Tuesday. I've attached the proposal and would like each of you to review it and send me any suggested changes by Friday afternoon.

Ellen Tuttle

Show Personal Interest

Effective managers make personal connections with their employees. E-mail allows managers to make such connections even when employees work at a distance.

Send a personal note when you feel it is appropriate, but make sure to keep the sentiments real and the details correct.

○ ○ ○   New Message   ⬭

To: (To: Myra Rosman)

Cc:

Subject: Congratulations on the Election!

Myra,

Congratulations on your election to the Uppsala Community Board. I'm delighted you can make this worthwhile contribution to your city. Your many skills and talents will make you an asset to that group just as you are an asset to our team.

Sincerely,

Bill Y.

International E-Mail

When you build international teams, remember that different cultures treat personal connections in different ways. For example, in Japan, managers often publicly praise teams for their accomplishments, while in Italy, managers usually praise individuals, and do so privately. Both cultures, however, value business partners that show deep respect. Being aware of these differences and similarities in cultures can help you make the strong connections with your international colleagues and clients.

"Do's and Don'ts" of E-Mail Management

E-mail can be abused like other tools of the business world. To avoid e-mail abuses, managers should remember the following key points.

Don't Rely on E-Mail Exclusively

Don't use e-mail as a substitute for personal interaction.

- Know when a personal discussion, meeting, or phone call will do a better job. E-mail is never as powerful as your physical presence.

- Handle major announcements in person.

- Never use e-mail to discipline an employee, handle a sensitive issue, or deliver bad news.

Do Police Yourself

Let all your employees know that e-mail is only as efficient as the person using it.

- Always read your e-mail before sending it, and revise when necessary.

- Be productive. Primarily use e-mail to do essential business.

Do Keep It Short

Keep most messages simple and to the point, respecting your employees' time.

- Make your subject line clear and compelling.

- Clearly identify your subject, context, priorities, and any action or follow-up that may be needed.

- Keep in mind that long messages often will not be read right away.

Do Distribute to a Short List

Send messages only to people who need them.

- Develop small distribution lists instead of large ones.

- Do not reply to the entire list if you really need to respond only to the sender.

Use Fair, Respectful Language

When managing via e-mail, always use fair, respectful language. The words you choose determine the impact you make on your readers. Always make sure your words avoid negative connotations with regard to gender, ethnicity, disability, and age.

- **Gender issues.** Be sure your language is gender neutral.

  - Avoid gender-specific references such as *mailman* or *chairman*. Use *mail carrier, chair* or *chairperson, police officer, firefighter*.

- **Race, religion, or ethnicity.** Nonspecific language respects the diversity of readers.

  - Avoid referring to religion or ethnicity unless it is an integral part of the message. When it is, use specific terms such as *Native American, African American, Jewish, Baptist*.

- **Disabilities.** Be aware of the preferred forms of references.

  - Avoid focusing on the disability instead of the person. Write *person with cancer* instead of *cancer sufferer*, and *disabled* rather than *handicapped*.

- **Age.** Don't use words with negative connotations.

  - Avoid focusing on the age instead of the person. Use *older adults* instead of *the aged*, and *youth* or *young people* instead of *kids* or *teens*.

FYI When you write, focus on the message, not the gender, culture, disability, or age of the person.

Section 2
The Traits of E-Mail Writing

in this section

3

Focus Your IDEAS

Whenever you have a bright idea, a well-written e-mail message can help you focus it. If your focus is strong enough, you may even light a fire under coworkers and clients!

A well-written e-mail has two types of bright ideas: a main point and supporting details. The main point tells readers why you are writing, and the supporting details empower the reader to take action. Turn to this chapter whenever you need to focus your ideas and write illuminating e-mails.

Your
Goal

Focus your main idea and select details.

3 Keys to Focused Ideas

1 Ask, "What do I want my reader to know?"

2 Select only necessary details.

3 Keep your message brief.

Q How do I focus my message?

One way to quickly focus your e-mail message is to ask, "Why am I writing?" The answer to that question is your purpose. Then ask yourself a second question, "What do I want the reader to know or do?" The answer to that question will be your focus.

Example

Purpose: To introduce the new orientation procedure to managers
Question: What do I want my reader to know or do?
Focus: The new orientation procedure will help the managers in two ways: (1) It will help the managers provide support for new employees, and (2) it will help the managers evaluate the employees' performance for six months.

Q How do I write a focus statement?

Use the formula below to write a statement that answers the question, "What do I want my reader to know or do?"

A specific topic
+ information or action
= focus statement

Example

The new orientation procedure will help the managers support and evaluate new employees.

Try It Use the question "What do I want my reader to know?" and write a focus statement for each main idea below.

1. **Purpose:** To thank a supplier whose prompt delivery kept our plant at full operation

2. **Purpose:** To notify employees that steps have been taken to correct the problems that yesterday's spot inspection uncovered

3. **Purpose:** To tell Dan Rivers that the company will not be able to hire the three production workers he requested

See sample answer on page 111.

Q How do I choose details to support my focus?

Select the details that best explain and support your main idea. The focus itself will help you choose relevant details for your e-mail—facts, statistics, 5 W's, observations, examples, anecdotes, and comparisons. The list below will help you to choose just the right details.

Facts ● Facts are pieces of information that can be proven to be true or accurate.
Always double-check your facts.

Statistics ● Statistics are collections of numerical facts or numbers.
Use precise numerical facts to prove a point.

5 W's ● The 5 W's are *Who? What? Where? When?* and *Why?* Use the 5 W's Chart on page 73.
Also use *H—How?*—when appropriate.

Observations ● When you pay close attention to people, places, things, events, and processes, you are collecting observations.
If you use observations, be certain they are fair and accurate. Don't "color" them with personal prejudices.

Examples ● Examples are items or instances that show how a whole category is similar.
Introduce examples with strong transitions. *See page 52.*

Anecdotes ● An anecdote is a short account of an incident. Using anecdotes helps you <u>show</u> your point instead of simply <u>telling</u> about it.
Describe physical characteristics of what was seen, heard, smelled, tasted, or felt. Include what happened to the people involved.

Comparisons ● Sometimes you need to show how two things are similar (comparison) or different (contrast).
Usually, you will put greater emphasis on either the differences or similarities.

Q How does the focus change for different readers?

The focus usually depends on the position of the reader. You will most likely write e-mail messages "up" to management, "down" to employees below you in the company's hierarchy, "across" to associates, or "out" to clients and customers.

Read the e-mails on the next two pages to see how three different focuses have been used for three different audiences. As you read, consider your position and your company. Ask yourself, "Would I use this same focus?" and "Would I choose the same details?"

An Employee Writing to a Supervisor

Purpose: To inform a supervisor about needed training
Question: What do I want my reader to know or do?
Focus: We need to budget for training our sales reps.

To:	Jim Perroni
Cc:	
Subject:	Spreadsheet Training for Sales Reps

New Message

Good Morning, Mr. Perroni:

Our regional managers are complaining about orders that are incorrectly filled due to poor spreadsheet skills among our sales force. I have researched training options:

• Upward Training offers on-site training in spreadsheet use, though this option is expensive and would require our sales force to gather in one location.

• Upward Training also offers online courses in spreadsheet use. These courses are more reasonable, and each rep could log on individually and work toward course certification.

To check out prices and course offerings, click this link:
http://www.UpwardandOnwardTraining.rr.us.

Please let me know if either of these options is acceptable. I would like to arrange some sort of training before the winter sales convention.

Thanks for your attention.

Oscar Willman

A Manager Writing to an Employee

Purpose: To temporarily turn down an employee's request for additional training

Question: What do I want my reader to know or do?

Focus: This is a good idea, and we will work to budget for it next year.

New Message

To: (Oscar Willman)

Cc:

Subject: Re: Spreadsheet Training for Sales Reps

Good Morning, Oscar:

Training is a good idea. You're right: Our sales reps do need to upgrade their technical skills to improve service. Thank you for including the link, which provided plenty of helpful information.

Unfortunately, the cost can't be built into this year's budget. However, because you have shown how important this training is, I will make it a priority for early next year.

Jim

To: (Juan Johns)

Cc: Oscar Willman

Subject: Budgeting for Spreadsheet Training

Dear Juan,

Next year, we need to budget for additional spreadsheet training. Our sales reps need training in order to eliminate the errors we are currently struggling with. I have attached an e-mail from Oscar Willman that outlines the need and the training options.

Thanks for your help.

Jim

A Manager Writing to Another Manager

Purpose: To inform the budget manager about needed funds

Question: What do I want my reader to know or do?

Focus: We need your help budgeting funds for training sales staff.

Q How can I understand each writing situation?

To understand any writing situation, you need to understand your purpose in writing, your audience (your reader), and the context of your message.

Purpose

Examine your reason for writing.

- Why am I writing?
- What do I want the reader to know?
- What do I want the reader to do?

Audience

Think about your reader and others involved in the situation.

- Who is my reader—superior, colleague, employee, client?
- What does the reader know?
- What does the reader need to know?
- What attitude will the reader have toward my message?
- Who else is involved?
- Who should be copied on this message?

Context

Describe the occasion for your e-mail.

- What is the story behind this e-mail—the situation in the company, in the field, and so on?
- Is this message part of a longer "thread" of exchanges? What is the thread?
- What might get in the way of my message being understood?
- When must the e-mail be sent?

> ## Try It
>
> Find a recent e-mail that you wrote to a supervisor. Rewrite the e-mail so that it is appropriate for an associate. Then choose an e-mail that you wrote to an associate and refocus it so it is appropriate for a supervisor. (Compare your e-mails to the models in this chapter.)

Improve Your ORGANIZATION

The writing trait "organization" may sound daunting, but it's really simple. Organization means getting all your ducks in a row. Your e-mail messages should start with the big duck (your main point) and let the little ducks (supporting details) follow it.

Whenever you need to put an e-mail in the best order, turn to this chapter for guidelines and graphic organizers.

Your Goal

Organize your message so that readers grasp it clearly and quickly.

4 Keys to Organization

1 Write a clear subject line.

2 Use the inverted-pyramid style for most e-mails.

3 Use special organization for bad-news or persuasive messages.

4 Use a graphic organizer.

Q Do I need to organize every e-mail I write?

You should organize your thoughts before you write even very short, routine e-mails. Since short e-mails often have only one paragraph, the first sentence usually states the focused main idea. Additional sentences contain the necessary details. A closing sentence may emphasize the main idea or make a statement about specific action that is needed.

Long e-mails may have several paragraphs and are usually harder to organize. Using graphic organizers can make the task manageable and the message clear.

> Making the simple complicated is commonplace; making the complicated simple, awesomely simple, that's creativity.
>
> Charles Mingus

Q Is the subject line a part of an e-mail's organization?

Yes, an e-mail uses a subject line to announce the main point of the message. An effective subject line is . . .

- **Precise**—Make the subject line specific and succinct.

  Write: Employee Career Options at Rankin

  Not: To offer our employees the opportunity to explore career options within Rankin Industries, both horizontally and vertically

- **Positive**—State the point of the message in positive or neutral terms.

  Write: Company Phone Policy Reminder

  Not: Warnings about abuse of company phone system

- **Relevant**—Let readers see how the subject relates to them.

  Write: Employee Career Options at Rankin

  Not: Career Options

- **Professional**—Use professional words and phrases.

  Write: Security Equipment Installation

  Not: Smile! We see you!

Activity 1: Use Clear, Informative Subject Lines (page 86)

Q Does an e-mail need a salutation or greeting?

A polite greeting is always welcome at the beginning of a message, and an e-mail that goes out to a client or customer must have one. For in-house e-mails, follow your company's policy or your supervisor's preference. To create a polite greeting, follow these tips:

- **Use a standard greeting.**

    Examples: Dear Team: Dear Ms. Jackson: Dear Elizabeth:

- **Use a less formal greeting for someone you know well.**

    Examples: Good Morning, Liz   Hello, Tom,   Hi!

Q Does an e-mail have a middle part?

Short e-mails may have only one main idea in one paragraph. Longer e-mails may have several main ideas and, therefore, several paragraphs that create a middle. Control the flow of information by putting each main point with its supporting details in a separate paragraph. If you are writing about one idea that has several parts, you may use separate paragraphs for each part.

Q Does an e-mail need a closing?

A polite closing is always appropriate at the end of an e-mail message, but follow your company's policy. If you want to thank a person or to request or offer help, do so in the line just before your name.

Examples: Thanks for the help,   Let me know!

International E-Mail

Some international e-mails are short and direct. They deliver very specific information that someone is expecting. (See page 83.) Other international e-mails resemble a letter and have a greeting and a closing. (See page 84.)

FYI
When you are sending a series of messages and responses back and forth, shape your opening sentence so it clearly links the previous comment to the comment you are about to make.

Q What is the best way to organize most messages?

When you are delivering good or neutral news, place your focus statement up front and provide details later. This organization plan is called the *inverted pyramid*. It ensures that the reader will grasp your most important point immediately.

When you use the inverted pyramid, you (1) write a general statement before giving specific examples, (2) give a summary before you provide details, (3) give an answer before an explanation, or (4) state a conclusion before including a discussion. *See the model on page 76.*

Focus Statement

Details

Example

The following e-mail uses the inverted pyramid as a method of organization. First, the writer states the conclusion, and then she offers an explanation.

○ ○ ○   New Message

To: (All Employees)

Cc:

Subject: New ID Card Security Policy

Good Morning, Everyone:

Effective immediately, all employees are required to swipe their company-issued ID cards to enter the workplace. Swipe terminals have been installed at each building entrance. Additionally, you must wear your clip-on ID cards at all times while on company premises.

Nameco is adopting this policy for your safety. Most of you are aware that the company experienced a significant theft last week as a result of an unknown person gaining access to one of the buildings. The new policy should help prevent such an event from recurring and help protect employees from intruders.

Each employee should already have an ID card issued by Human Resources. If you have misplaced the card, please see Ms. Harding in Human Resources for a replacement.

Thanks for your cooperation,

Jana Oates

Activity 2: Use an Inverted Pyramid (page 87)

Q How can organization help me deliver bad news?

When you are presenting unexpected bad news, you should not begin with your focus statement (the bad news). Instead, start with a buffer—a statement that offers agreement, understanding, or appreciation. Then provide an explanation that leads to your focus statement. Afterward, exit gracefully.

Note: If the bad news is expected, you can break the news gently up front.

Buffer

Explanation

Bad News (Focus Statement)

Exit

Example

The following e-mail expresses appreciation, explains the issue, provides the bad news, and exits by emphasizing the future.

○ ○ ○   New Message

To: (David Jenkins)

Cc:

Subject: Print-on-Demand Update

Dear David:

I greatly appreciate your researching the print-on-demand option for our in-service trainings. You are right that these events take a heavy toll on our copiers and take a lot of time for employee trainers. However, even figuring in these costs, the print-on-demand option still is prohibitively expensive. We'll keep watching the market and see if this trend changes.

Thanks for your hard work, and let me know if you find a more economical print-on-demand service.

Best regards,

Rob Koenig

Q How can organization help me persuade?

When you are trying to persuade your reader, don't start with your focus: "Buy my product." Doing so may sound pushy or disrespectful. Instead, capture the reader's attention, build interest and desire, and then call the reader to action with your focus statement.

You can capture your reader's attention by mentioning a problem and offering a solution, by starting with good news and connecting it to your point, or by starting with the reader's idea and leading to your own.

Attention

Interest and Desire

Action (Focus Statement)

Example

The following e-mail catches the reader's attention by addressing a problem and offering a solution. It builds interest and desire before delivering a call to action (a command).

	New Message
To:	Marcia Tilzow
Cc:	
Subject:	Finding Another Copywriter

Dear Marcia:

I heard that President Reynolds turned down our request to hire a new copywriter, citing our tight budget and intermittent schedule. I have a suggestion that could get us the help we need when we need it.

I suggest we hire interns from Randle College, which has a strong business department. The students would work economically, getting course credit for their work, and they could help us during our summer and winter crunches, when they are not in school. Follow this link to find out more about the internship program at Randle College. http://www.randlecollege.rr.us.org./intern/.

Thanks!

Steven Smith

Q What types of graphic organizers work well?

T-bars and time lines are particularly useful for organizing e-mails. To see how you can use these to write e-mails, turn to pages 77, 79, and 82. In that section, you will also find additional graphic organizers like the Venn diagram and a 5 W's chart. Use these models and the activities to help you become familiar with graphic organizers.

T-Bar

The T-bar is a two-column chart that can be used to organize many different kinds of messages. For example, if the subject is "New Sick-Leave Policy," the columns could be labeled "Costs" and "Benefits," or "Pros" and "Cons," or "Major Considerations" and "Other Considerations." T-bars are especially useful because of their flexibility. *See the e-mail models on pages 77 and 84.*

T-Bar

Subject: New Sick-Leave Policy

Topic: Costs	**Topic:** Benefits
• Point 1	• Point 1
• Point 2	• Point 2
• Point 3	• Point 3

Time Line

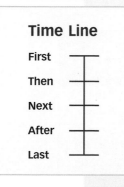

Time Line

First
Then
Next
After
Last

A time line is another graphic organizer that can help you organize your thinking on a number of key issues: Have you included all the steps? Do you have the steps listed in proper order? Do you need to list some details under each step? A time line helps you answer these kinds of questions and picture the entire process before you begin to write. *See the models on pages 79 and 82.*

Q How can lists help me organize my message?

Lists help both the writer and the reader quickly see the details. If there is sequence or ranking to your lists, use numbers. If the order *isn't* important, use bullets or asterisks to separate the details. *Refer to the model lists on pages 72, 75, 80, and 83.*

List

1st Main Point
- Detail
- Detail
- Detail

2nd Main Point
- Detail
- Detail
- Detail

List

When creating a list, phrase the items in a parallel way. This means beginning each point with the same grammatical form. For example, if you want to list job duties, you might set them up in the following ways:

Your duties include:	*or*	You will be expected to:
• Collect**ing** test results.		• **Collect** test results.
• Fil**ing** the results.		• **File** the results.
• Respond**ing** to client inquiries.		• **Respond** to client inquiries.

Try It Rewrite the following e-mail. Use either a bulleted list or a numbered list.

To: All Employees

This is just a reminder to everyone. Last weekend, the coffeepot in one of the departments was left on. The coffee boiled away. This ruined the carafe and could have caused a fire. If you work over the weekend, please remember to unplug the coffeepot. In addition, if you are the last to leave your area, please shut down your computer and turn off the copier. Also, please remember to turn out the lights in both the main area and the restrooms, and check to see if the night phones are on.

Activity 7: Write Parallel Lists (page 92)

See sample revision on page 111.

5

Use an Appropriate VOICE

Have you ever shouted from a mountaintop? Whatever voice you use comes right back to you. If you shout a friendly greeting, that's what you receive. If you shout an angry phrase, you'll get it right back.

E-mail works the same way. Use a professional, courteous voice, and you'll probably get a professional, courteous reply. If you sound angry and unprofessional, expect the same to come back to you. This chapter will help you create a voice that reflects well on you and your company.

Your Goal

Write with an appropriate voice for your reader.

4 Keys to Appropriate Voice

1. Know your reader.

2. Use a professional voice.

3. Make your voice sound personal when possible.

4. Write as you would speak to your reader.

Q How does an unprofessional voice sound?

An unprofessional voice sounds rude, negative, and disrespectful. Read the e-mail below and note the unprofessional voice used. The numbered items point out problem areas.

○ ○ ○   New Message

To: (Al Henderson)

Cc:

Subject: Where Are Your Evaluation Forms?!

Henderson: (1)

I see that you (2) are late with your line evaluation forms again. Your personal problems (3) have resulted in an inability to perform your duties and are cutting down G sector's efficiency, putting us all behind schedule. Such laziness is beyond acceptable parameters (4) and will not be tolerated. Get on the ball or get out. (5)

Your supervisor,

T. Frederick Behr

Try It

Rewrite the e-mail message, making it sound professional. Then compare your message with the one you see on the next page. How well did you do?

What makes this message sound unprofessional?

1 Using the last name as a greeting is rude.

2 This use of *you* sounds disrespectful and accusatory.

3 This personal reference lacks tact and common courtesy.

4 The use of "big" words is unnecessary.

5 The overall tone is negative and harsh.

Q How does a professional voice sound?

A professional voice sounds specific, positive, and reasonable. Read the e-mail below and note the professional voice.

○○○   New Message   ▭

To: (Al Henderson)

Cc:

Subject: Reminder About Evaluation Forms

Dear Al:

I just wanted to remind you to turn in your line evaluation forms from last week. (1) Your division has always been a top performer (2) but has been a little off lately, (3) and these forms will help us monitor where we can help you improve efficiency. (4)

If there is any way I can help, please let me know. (5)

Sincerely,

T. Frederick Behr

What makes this message sound professional?

1 A specific action is requested.

2 A positive aspect is emphasized.

3 A reason is given for the concern.

4 Tact is used instead of blame—the "we" indicates a partnership.

5 The sender adopts a supportive tone.

Try It
Rewrite each of the following sentences to create a more professional voice.

1. You understood about half of the points I presented at the meeting.
2. You lost the bid.
3. Try not to mess up this project like you did the last one.
4. Your loan rates are going up next month.

See sample answers on page 113.

Q What is a personal voice, and when should I use it?

A personal voice—used more and more in business communication—is a direct voice using personal pronouns such as *you, I, we, us, yours, mine,* and *ours.*

Example

Avoid: Client communications must create a positive corporate image.

Write: **Your** communications with **our** clients give **our** company the positive image **we** want to build.

Business people use the personal voice to support, influence, or persuade other people. The inclusive nature of the personal voice causes others to feel that they are a part of the team. Choose this voice when problem solving, collaborating, or building a relationship with associates, clients, and customers.

Example

Avoid: Supplying industrial diamonds to important customers of many years remains our goal.

Write: **We** have been **your** supplier of industrial diamonds since 1963, and **we** want to continue to be **your** supplier for at least another 40 years. It is **our** privilege to serve **you**.

International E-Mail Appropriate Voice

Different cultures use different voices. Low-context countries like the United States and Germany use a direct voice. France and England are more high-context, and information is not communicated as directly. China and Japan are even higher-context countries, and they appreciate implied messages. Before spending a lot of time wondering about how direct or indirect to be, use the following guidelines to create an acceptable voice.

1. **Be respectful.**
2. **Keep an open mind as you send and receive messages.**
3. **Always be honest.**
4. **Show you are a thoughtful, concerned person.**

FYI

Use the following guidelines to create an appropriate professional voice.

- **Be sincere.** Say what you mean and mean what you say.
- **Be courteous.** Imagine you are receiving the message.
- **Be upbeat.** Focus on solutions, improvements, and gratitude.
- **Be tactful.** Focus on the issues, not the people. Don't place blame.

Q How do I get to "know" my reader?

When you are writing or responding to an e-mail, imagine yourself in your reader's position. This helps you write with an appropriate and sincere voice. If you are writing to someone for the first time, use the following questions to help you get a picture of your reader.

- What does my reader already know about this subject?

- What does the person need to know?

- How will my reader react to this message?

- Do I want the person to do something? What?

- Am I writing "up" to management, "down" to other employees, "across" to associates, or "out" to customers and suppliers?

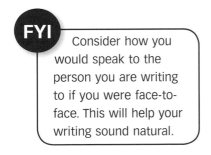

FYI Consider how you would speak to the person you are writing to if you were face-to-face. This will help your writing sound natural.

Q How do I create different voices?

You create different voices by changing your level of language. Your e-mail voice can be formal, informal, or conversational. Study the chart below to see characteristics of different voices.

What Kind of Voice Is It?		
	Characteristics	*Example*
Formal	• No contractions • Few personal pronouns • Objective words • Specific terminology	**As previously indicated, Klaar Corporation appreciates serving your clients in the Newark area.**
Informal	• Friendly, but professional • Occasional contractions and personal pronouns	**We've enjoyed working with your clients in the Newark area.**
Conversational	• Frequent contractions • Appropriate humor • Some jargon or slang	**Your Newark customers are the best!**

Q How do I tailor my voice to write "up" to management?

When you write to superiors, use a formal voice. Below and on the next page are examples of two e-mails giving the same message. One of the recipients is the writer's supervisor; the other is a coworker. Compare these e-mails.

Formal Voice

```
○ ○ ○                    New Message                          ⬭

  To:   ( dcwelles@wellescorp.com )

  Cc:

Subject:   Progress of Blue Springs Development Project (1)
```

Dear Ms. Welles: (2)

As a member of the team working on the Blue Springs Development project, you will be happy that we have come to an agreement with the plumbing contractor, and the project is back on track. I wanted to keep you informed about our progress, and I will provide a full report at our division meeting on Monday at 9:00 a.m. (3)

Thank you for your continued support on this project.

Kim Song (4)

Project Manager

FYI The voice you use in business e-mails depends on the topic and your relationship with the person receiving the message. However, when sending any messages that could be forwarded or read by others, use a professional, respectful tone.

What makes this e-mail appropriate for management?

1 The subject line clearly explains what the message is about.

2 The greeting is formal.

3 The language is formal and respectful.

4 The closing includes not only the sender's name but her title as well.

Q How do I tailor my voice to write "across" to an associate?

When you write to coworkers, your voice can be more conversational. The message below deals with the same topic as the message on page 38, but the voice is more casual.

Conversational Voice

○ ○ ○	New Message
To:	(jfernandez@wellescorp.com)
Cc:	
Subject:	Blue Springs (1)

Well, Joan, we did it! (2)

The plumbing contractor has finally come around, and soon the water will flow in Blue Springs. Thanks for all the extra hours (and cups of coffee) it took to make it all work. Get some sleep this weekend, and we'll all celebrate further at Monday's 9:00 a.m. meeting. (3)

Thanks again, (4)

Kim

Try It

Select an e-mail you have sent to a superior and rewrite the information as though you were sending it to a coworker. Next, find a conversational e-mail and rewrite it as if you were sending it to your supervisor. What changes do you make? Is the voice of each piece appropriate for the new recipient?

What makes this e-mail appropriate for an associate?

1 The subject refers to the project but is more casual.

2 An informal greeting includes the recipient's name.

3 The message is lighter and suggests a closeness between the sender and recipient.

4 The closing is brief and friendly, with the sender's first name only.

Q How do I tailor my voice to write to a subordinate?

When writing to motivate workers, to inform them about goals, to explain new policies or product lines, and to build goodwill and teamwork, use an informal voice. Sincerity and politeness are important in the memos and reports that flow to subordinates.

Informal Voice

```
◯ ◯ ◯                        New Message                          ▭

      To:  ( Estelle )

      Cc:

  Subject:   Letter to Ralph Rodriquez About Code Compliance
```

Good Morning, Estelle: (1)

The plumbing contractor has agreed to the installation of sump pumps in the houses that are part of the Blue Springs Development. Please draft a letter to Inspector #78, Ralph Rodriquez, at City Hall to tell him that we have made arrangements to meet Code 1295.78. (2)

Also, please ask Harold to adjust the cost-balance sheet before Monday's 9:00 a.m. meeting. The estimated cost of the pumps and labor is $7,155. The work is to be completed by November 15. (3)

Finally, please make arrangements for any necessary changes to the promotional documents for the houses. Thanks for your help. If you have questions or run into a problem, e-mail or call me. (4)

Kim

What makes this e-mail appropriate for a subordinate?

1 The writer uses a friendly greeting.
2 She gives needed information.
3 She is polite and direct.
4 She offers support.

Try It
Compose appropriate e-mails for these topics.

1. A request for project assistance *(to a coworker)*
2. A request for project assistance or more funding *(to a supervisor)*
3. A request for assistance from a subordinate
See sample answers on page 113.

6

Choose WORDS with Care

"That galaxy is hyperplastic." Huh? "The galaxy is huge." Ah! Word choice can make all the difference between a message that communicates and one that obfuscates (confuses).

The best e-mail messages use natural, common language and avoid technical words and jargon. This chapter will help you find the very best words to use in your e-mail messages.

Your
Goal

- Choose words that make your message clear, concise, and natural sounding.

4 Keys to Effective Word Choice

1 Avoid unnecessary adjectives and adverbs.

2 Use specific words.

3 Avoid technical words and jargon.

4 Choose words that sound natural.

Q What do I need to know about modifiers?

You should cut unnecessary adjectives and adverbs. Redundant modifiers annoy readers and make writing sound puffed up. The chart below shows some unnecessary adjectives and adverbs that should be cut from your writing.

DON'T WRITE	WRITE
Let me provide my **personal** opinion.	Let me provide my opinion.
Talks will soon resume **again**.	Talks will soon resume.
Claire **first** originated the idea.	Claire originated the idea.
We appreciate your **mutual** cooperation.	We appreciate your cooperation.
Ed outlined our **final** conclusions.	Ed outlined our conclusions.

Q What do I need to know about "little modifiers"?

Some little modifiers can make you sound uncertain about your feelings, thoughts, or observations. The list below is a sample of these words. "Little modifiers" also weaken your sentences and your attempts at being persuasive.

a bit	quite	kind of	sort of	very
a little	pretty much	rather	in a sense	too

Q How do I know what the "right" word is?

Watch for easily confused words—*to, too,* or *two; their, there,* or *they're; affect, effect; accept, except; amount, number;* and many more. Make a list of confusing words and use a dictionary or grammar book to check the usage. The activities below will help you learn more about word usage.

Activity 8: Use Adjectives and Adverbs with Care (page 93)
Activity 10: Use the Right Word (page 95)

Q What do I need to know about verbs and nouns?

You need to know that active verbs give your writing energy and momentum, and specific nouns make your writing precise. Bottom line: Use active verbs and specific nouns.

Examples

Weak: The lead guy was let go.

Strong: The CEO of Ebbing Labs resigned today.
The board of directors fired CEO Romney today.

Weak: The equipment doesn't do a good job.

Strong: The power washer lacks the pressure needed to
remove dried material from the mixer walls.

FYI

Study the nouns and verbs in the chart below. Note how each becomes more specific as you move to the right.

people	employees	engineers
put	added	inserted
an amount	dollars	$1,000
next week	January 12	January 12, 3:00

Try It Use specific words to make the following message clear and precise.

Tomorrow all supervisors in the Sales Department will meet to discuss several problems. *See sample answer on page 113.*

Activity 9: Choose Specific Verbs and Nouns (page 94)

Q How do I avoid technical words and jargon?

Use plain English instead of "technospeak" or "business speak," both of which are full of technical or professional jargon. Although you might need to use technical language when communicating with other professionals, general business communication should avoid technical words and jargon.

Examples

Business Speak: We expect all personnel, from regular to ancillary, to follow established protocol, thus ensuring benchmark compliance.

Plain English: We expect all employees to follow established policies and to honor company standards.

Try It Rewrite each of the following sentences, using plain English.

1. You can obtain the new software with no <u>up front monetary outlay</u>.
2. We are <u>cognizant of the fact</u> that you have requested an extension.
3. <u>It is our intention to terminate</u> Columbus Day as a paid holiday.
4. This will <u>precipitate a paradigm</u> shift in our production schedule.
5. We will need time to <u>recapitulate</u> our position and plan strategies.
6. We will have to <u>utilize whatever modifications are necessitated to obtain the wherewithal</u> to restructure our department. *See sample answers on page 113.*

International E-Mail **Avoid Idioms**

Idioms are groups of words whose meaning might not be understood by all individuals. Avoid idioms when communicating with persons who are non-native speakers of English. Use the "meaning" as shown below, instead of the idiom.

Idiom	*Meaning*
beat around the bush	**avoid getting to the point**
chicken feed	**not worth much money**
food for thought	**something to think about**
in a nutshell	**summarized**
in the black	**making money**
in the red	**in debt**

Activity 11:
Avoid Idioms
(page 96)

Q How can I make my writing sound natural?

Use plain, simple language. The list below shows the difference between words and phrases that sound natural and those that sound forced and unnatural.

Unnatural	Natural
accordingly	so
according to our records	our records show
acquaint	inform
adhere	stick
afford an opportunity	allow/permit
along the lines of	like
apprise	tell
are in receipt of	have received
are of the opinion	think
ascertain	learn/find out
as per	according to
as regards	regarding
awaiting your instructions	please let me know
be applicable to	apply to
call your attention to	please note
case in point	example
ceased functioning	quit working
cognizant	aware
commence	begin
concur	agree
configuration	shape
disbursements	payments
do not hesitate to	please
due consideration	careful thought
endeavor	try
enumerate	list
evacuate	leave
expedite	speed up
fabricate	make
facilitate	make easier
finalize	settle/finish
fluctuate	vary
herein	in this
heretofore	until now
in accordance with	as

Unnatural	Natural
inasmuch as	as/because
increment	amount/step
indispensable	vital
in lieu of	instead of
in the amount of	for
kindly	please
manifest	show
manipulate	operate
modification	change
necessitate	require
on a daily basis	daily
paradigm shift	major change
parameter	limit
per se	as such
personnel reduction	layoffs
per your request	as requested
precipitate	cause
preliminary to	before
prioritize	rank
procure	buy/get
pursuant to	following up
quantify	measure/count
ramification	result
recapitulate	review
remuneration	pay
reproduction	copy
salient	important
strategize	plan/solve
subsequent	later/after
terminate	end
under separate cover	separately
utilize	use
vacillate	waver
visualize	picture
wherewithal	means

Q How can I make my writing concise?

Avoid saying the same thing twice. Instead, use concise words that deliver your message quickly and clearly. The following list will help you write more concisely.

Wordy	Concise	Wordy	Concise
advance forward	**advance**	for the reasons that	**because**
advance planning	**planning**	free gift	**gift**
a majority of	**most**	free of charge	**free**
any and all	**all**	having the capacity to	**can**
are of the opinion that	**believe**	in light of the fact that	**since**
ask the question	**ask**	in order to	**to**
assembled together	**assembled**	in the amount of	**for**
at an early date	**soon**	in the event that	**if**
attach together	**attach**	it is often the case that	**often**
at the conclusion of	**after/following**	it is our opinion that	**we believe that**
at the present time	**now**	it is our recommendation	**we recommend**
basic essentials	**essentials**	it is our understanding	**we understand**
both together	**together**	join together	**join**
brief in duration	**brief**	joint partnership	**partnership**
close in proximity	**close**	make reference to	**refer to**
combine together	**combine**	meet together	**meet**
completely unanimous	**unanimous**	mutual cooperation	**cooperation**
consensus of opinion	**consensus**	on a daily basis	**daily**
descend down	**descend**	on a weekly basis	**weekly**
despite the fact that	**although**	over again	**again**
disregard altogether	**disregard**	personal in nature	**personal**
due to the fact that	**because**	personal opinion	**opinion**
during the course of	**during**	pertaining to	**about**
end result	**result**	plan ahead	**plan**
few in number	**few**	postponed until later	**postponed**
filled to capacity	**filled**	prior to	**before**
final outcome	**outcome**	repeat again	**repeat**
foreign imports	**imports**	until such time as	**until**
for the purpose of	**for**	with regard to	**about**

Improve Your **SENTENCES**

No matter how you measure it, a square peg doesn't fit in a round hole. In the same way, there's a perfect size and shape of sentence for every idea you want to express. Most ideas work best in sentences that are 20 words or fewer. Really big ideas might need even more words—as long as the thought remains clear. This chapter will help you write sentences that are just the right size and shape to fit your ideas.

Your **Goal**

• Write clear, precise sentences.

5 Keys to Improving Sentences

1 **Write complete sentences.**

2 **Use active voice.**

3 **Divide long or rambling sentences.**

4 **Combine choppy sentences.**

5 **Use transitions.**

Q How do I combine choppy sentences?

Short, choppy sentences sound abrupt and disconnected. They often give all ideas equal treatment, even though key points need emphasis. Use the following suggestions to combine and connect choppy sentences.

Use a series. When you have several related ideas or details, you can use a series to create one sentence.

> **Choppy:**   The adjuster examined the roof. She checked the valleys closely. She also inspected the carport.
>
> **Combined:**   The adjuster examined the roof, checked the valleys closely, and inspected the carport.

Use a coordinating conjunction. Join sentences with the conjunctions *and, but, or, nor, for, yet,* or *so.* These conjunctions show equal relationships between ideas and details.

> **Choppy:**   Damon is a repair specialist. He can repair landing gears and brakes.
>
> **Combined:**   Damon is a repair specialist, so he can repair landing gears and brakes.

Use a subordinating conjunction. Join sentences with conjunctions such as *although, before, in order that, unless,* and *while.* These conjunctions show that one idea is more important than another.

> **Choppy:**   I work at United Medical. I have trained more than 200 people in health-care systems.
>
> **Combined:**   While working at United Medical (*less important idea*), I have trained more than 200 people in health-care systems (*more important idea*).

Activity 16: Combine Choppy Sentences (page 101)
Activity 17: Edit Choppy Sentences (page 102)

Q How do I fix run-on sentences?

A run-on sentence is actually two sentences joined incorrectly. Run-ons confuse your reader and detract from your message. You can use one of three techniques to fix a run-on sentence.

Run-On: The latest report on the progress of the HT Project fails to figure in the effect of employee vacations and the brief electrical malfunction of the 24th the report appears incomplete.

Corrected: 1. **Use a period.** Place a period after _**24th**_ and capitalize _**the**_.
2. **Use a semicolon.** Place a semicolon (;) after _**24th**_.
3. **Use a comma and a coordinating conjunction.** Place a comma after _**24th**_ and add a coordinating conjunction: _and, so_.

Q Why use transitions to connect sentences?

Transitions show your reader how the ideas in your sentences link or relate to each other. See the list of transitions on page 52.

Unrelated: The proposal from Rankin Industries includes the cost of inside wiring. It does not include costs for speakers. The proposal from Taylor Industries includes both costs.

Related: The proposal from Rankin Industries includes the cost of inside wiring, **but** it does not include costs for speakers. **However**, the proposal from Taylor Industries includes both costs.

Try It Rewrite the following paragraph, using transitions to connect the short, choppy sentences. (See the chart on page 52 for help selecting transitions.)

I will be happy to start work on August 24. I'll begin to search for housing. Thank you for the material you sent about moving costs and real estate agencies. Could you please send information about area schools?
See sample answer on page 114.

Activity 18: Fix Run-On Sentences (page 103)
Activity 19: Use Transitions and Key Words (page 104)

Q What transitions work well?

Transitions show how ideas are linked by location, time, comparison, and so on. Transitions link sentences and paragraphs into an easy-to-read document.

Words That Show Location

above	away from	between	in front of	onto	to the right
across	behind	beyond	inside	on top of	under
along	below	by	into	outside	
among	beneath	down	near	over	
around	beside	in back of	off	throughout	

Words That Show Time

about	as soon as	first	next	then	tomorrow
after	before	immediately	next week	third	until
afterward	during	later	second	till	when
again	finally	meanwhile	soon	today	yesterday

Words That Compare Things (Show Similarities)

also	as	in the same way	like	likewise	similarly

Words That Contrast Things (Show Differences)

although	even though	in contrast	on the other hand	still
but	however	nevertheless	otherwise	yet

Words That Emphasize a Point

actually	for this reason	the main point	to repeat
again	in fact	to emphasize	truly

Words That Conclude, Summarize, Recommend

all in all	because	in conclusion	therefore
as a result	finally	in summary	to sum up

Words That Add Information

additionally	also	as well	for example	likewise
again	and	besides	for instance	moreover
along with	another	finally	in addition	next

Words That Clarify

for example	for instance	in other words	put another way	that is

8

Check for **CORRECT COPY**

During a routine checkup, you may feel fine, but your doctor is still likely to check your vital signs: heartbeat, blood pressure, and breathing. You won't be released until your doctor is sure you are healthy.

Before you release an e-mail, you should check its vital signs, too: punctuation, capitalization, spelling, and grammar. Correct messages reflect your professionalism and your commitment to quality. This chapter will help you gain a healthy respect for correct copy!

Your
Goal
● Write error-free e-mails.

5 Keys to Correct Copy

1 Use commas correctly.

2 Make subjects and verbs agree.

3 Make pronouns and antecedents agree.

4 Check use of apostrophes.

5 Check for other common errors.

Q How can I use commas correctly?

<u>Use commas to</u> . . .

- **set off introductory word groups.**

    Since the beginning of the project, we have had confidence in its successful completion.

    Although the two committees initially agreed, they now have different interpretations.

    Thinking the weather reports were false, I did not wear a coat.

- **join two sentences with a coordinating conjunction** (*and, but, for, or, so, yet, nor*)**.**

    The financial backing has been generous, so our child care center opens tomorrow.

- **set off all nonessential or explanatory elements.**

    The team leader, along with everyone else involved, is to be complimented on a seamless operation.

- **set apart two or more adjectives that equally modify the same noun.**

    We look forward to a swift, satisfactory result.

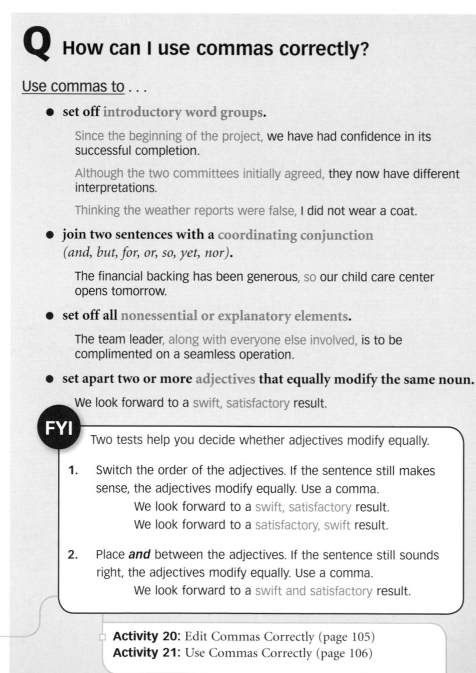

FYI

Two tests help you decide whether adjectives modify equally.

1. Switch the order of the adjectives. If the sentence still makes sense, the adjectives modify equally. Use a comma.

    We look forward to a swift, satisfactory result.
    We look forward to a satisfactory, swift result.

2. Place **and** between the adjectives. If the sentence still sounds right, the adjectives modify equally. Use a comma.

    We look forward to a swift and satisfactory result.

Activity 20: Edit Commas Correctly (page 105)
Activity 21: Use Commas Correctly (page 106)

Q When do I use commas with a clause?

The use of commas with clauses depends on whether the clause is restrictive or nonrestrictive.

- **When a clause is** nonrestrictive**, or <u>not</u> <u>needed</u> to understand the sentence,** use commas**.**

    The announcement, which was sent out yesterday, informed employees of a new insurance plan. *(We do <u>not</u> <u>need</u> the clause to understand what was announced.)*

- **When a clause is** restrictive**, which means it is <u>needed</u> to understand the sentence,** no commas **are used.**

    The announcement that was sent out yesterday contained some errors. *(We <u>do</u> <u>need</u> the clause to understand which announcement contained errors.)*

Try It Check your use of commas. Place commas in the following sentences.

1. Although the front-end loader was adequate when we began we now need something larger.

2. The shipment was late and when the materials did arrive they were broken.

3. Could you along with two or three workers from your department attend the seminar?

4. Roy who is training to be a supervisor is an asset to our service department.

5. Companies that offer flexible hours usually have happier more efficient workers.

See sample answers on page 118.

Q How can I be sure my subjects agree with their verbs?

Check any sentence that has a compound subject or a collective noun as the subject. The information below will help you choose verbs for those sentences.

Compound Subjects

When you have a **compound subject** where one subject is singular and one is plural, your verb will depend on the coordinating conjunction between those subjects.

- **If the conjunction is "and," the verb must be plural.**

   The workers and supervisor agree on the new contract.

   The supervisor and the workers agree on the new contract.

- **If the conjunction is "or" or "nor," the verb must agree with the subject nearest to it.**

   Either the supervisor or the workers agree on the new contract.

   Neither the workers nor the supervisor agrees on the new contract.

Collective Nouns

Collective nouns like *team, committee, group, government,* or *family* most often use a singular verb.

   The team makes good decisions.

However, if the **collective noun** is referring to individuals, then a plural verb is used.

   His team are mostly accountants and salespeople.

Yet, it is best to avoid this issue by rewriting the sentence.

   The members of his team are mostly accountants and salespeople.

   His team members are mostly accountants and salespeople.

Try It Change the verbs to agree with the subjects.

1. Neither the board nor our stockholders wants to delay the merger.

2. Ms. Roberts and Mr. Dayton wishes to use the mediation system.

3. Either the complainants or the union representative give the final approval.

4. The committee vote on issues like that one.

5. Our customers and the supplier needs our immediate attention.

6. The company's CEO and the union makes good decisions.

See sample answers on page 118.

Activity 22: Check Subject-Verb Agreement (page 107)

Q How do I make pronouns and antecedents agree?

- **Pronouns** and their antecedents must agree in number. They must both be singular or both be plural.

> The participants agreed that they found the meeting informative.

> Each participant agreed that he or she found the meeting informative.

- **Pronouns** and their antecedents must also agree in gender.

> Ms. Reynolds said that she learned much about the new routing system.

> Bill said that he learned much about the new routing system.

FYI

Using **he or she** and **his or her** is cumbersome. If possible, rewrite the sentence. Make the antecedent plural and use **they** and **their**.

Instead of . . .
A participant will learn how to file his or her e-mail.

Use . . .
Participants will learn how to file their e-mails.

Try It Select a pronoun for each blank. The first one has been done for you.

Our visitors from Taiwan enjoyed (1) __*their*__ tour of the factory. (2) _____ commented favorably about Mrs. Winston, the guide. It appears that (3) _____ was thorough and interesting. I would like to recommend that we send Mrs. Winston a note expressing (4) _____ thanks for (5) _____ excellent representation of our company.

See sample answers on page 118.

☐ **Activity 23:** Check Pronoun-Antecedent Agreement (page 108)

Q What else do I need to know about using pronouns?

The two hints below will help you use pronouns effectively.

- **Place a pronoun as close as possible to its antecedent. This makes sentences clear.**

  Clear: The sales report and the inventory report were published today. **They** showed a large profit, and all departments were pleased.

  Unclear: The sales report and the inventory report were published today. All departments were pleased to see that *they* showed a large profit. (Does *they* refer to the reports or the departments?)

- **Repeat a word instead of using a pronoun in sentences with two possible antecedents.**

  Clear: Mr. Busby hired Mr. Timms. Mr. Timms will replace Ms. Neki, who retired.

  Unclear: Mr. Busby hired Mr. Timms. **He** will replace Ms. Neki, who retired. (Will Mr. Busby or Mr. Timms replace Ms. Neki?)

Try It Correct errors in pronoun-antecedent or subject-verb agreement. After you change a pronoun, check to see if you now need to change a verb.

   Ms. Prentice of the IT Department have requested that each employee monitor his or her e-mail for spam messages. They further state that there is a computer virus infecting the area. All employees should be aware that his or her computers is at risk. The antivirus software installed on your computer should be checked. The software can be run by clicking on the icons that appears on the desktop.

See sample answers on page 118.

Q When should I use apostrophes?

Remember that apostrophes are used most often to show who owns something (to show possession) and to form contractions. They are also used to form plurals.

To show possession.

- The possessive of a singular noun is usually made by adding an apostrophe and *s*.

    person's ideas
    pipe's fitting
    motor's sound

- The plural possessive is formed by adding an apostrophe after the final *s*.

    Several persons' thoughts
    two pipes' fittings
    many motors' sounds

- To show possession shared by more than one noun, add the apostrophe and *s* to the last noun in the series.

    Nora, Tim, and Oscar's idea

- If possession is individual and not shared, add the possessive form to each of the nouns in the series.

    Nora's, Tim's, and Oscar's ideas

To form contractions.

- An apostrophe is used to replace dropped letters in contractions.

    cannot = can't   they have = they've

- When numbers are left out, an apostrophe indicates the omission.

    bear market of '92

To form plurals in special cases.

- An apostrophe and *s* are used to form the plural of a letter, a number, or a sign.

    A's   6's and 7's   #'s

- Use an apostrophe and *s* to form the plural of a word that is referred to as a word.

    "Don't give me any if's, and's or but's."

Activity 24: Use Apostrophes Correctly (page 109)
Activity 25: Edit Apostrophes Correctly (page 110)

Q Do I need to avoid nouns made from verbs?

Some writers have a habit of turning verbs into nouns. While not incorrect, the nouns made from verbs are weak, and using them often makes a sentence wordy. Whenever possible, use strong verbs—not a noun made from the verb—to get your point across clearly and concisely.

Weak Noun . . .	Strong Verb . . .
Ms. Cois gave a **presentation** about the report.	Ms. Cois **presented** the report.
Our team made a **decision** to get more input.	Our team **decided** to get more input.
He gave a **suggestion** for a solution.	He **suggested** a solution.
We sent out an **announcement** about our plans yesterday.	We **announced** our plans yesterday.

Try It Use verbs to eliminate nouns made from verbs and rewrite the following sentences.

1. Mr. Kramer's subsequent surgeries caused paralyzation.
2. Ms. Johnson's discussion was about living conditions in rural China.
3. The object caused an obstruction in his esophagus.
4. Mr. Landis's inspiration made us work harder.
5. Security conducted an investigation after the break-in.
6. His answer was a surprise to me.
7. The children's performance entertained us all.

See sample answers on page 118.

Q What other problems should I avoid?

Among the most common problems you will want to avoid is the misuse of "hopefully." Don't start a sentence with "hopefully." Instead, use phrases such as "I hope that" or "We are hopeful."

Use third person pronouns when you use third person nouns.

Often business writers use the third person. Third person pronouns are *he, she, it, they, his, hers, their*. Don't shift to the second person pronoun *you*. (If you write about yourself, use first person and pronouns such as *I, we, mine, ours*.)

Make sure your verbs establish a dominant tense.

Use a Dominant Tense
Our team **meets** (**present tense**) every Tuesday morning. Someone **brings** (**present tense**) donuts for all of us, and we **brainstorm** (**present tense**) ideas for new products. Next Tuesday we **will suggest** (**future tense**) names for the new soap.

Avoid Using Mixed Verb Tenses
Our team **meets** (**present tense**) every Tuesday morning. Someone **brought** (**past tense**) donuts for all of us, and we **will brainstorm** (**future tense**) ideas for new products. Next Tuesday we **will have suggested** (**future perfect tense**) names for the new soap.

Correct: Young **professionals** work in big cities where **they** find the music, comedy, and other entertainment **they** like.

Incorrect: Young professionals work in big cities where you find the music, comedy, and other entertainment you like.

Be good, do well.

"Good" is an adjective used to describe a person, place, or thing.

It's a good thing.
He enjoys good health.
We did a good job.

"Well" is an adverb used to describe a verb.
They did well.
How well can you write?

Avoid incorrect substitutions.

Use: Try to go.
Avoid: Try and go.

Use: I would have gone.
Avoid: I would of gone.

Q What other things make my writing better?

Keep things parallel

Whenever you use a series of words or phrases, use the same grammatical form.

Poor Writing The technicians <u>checked</u> the virus software, <u>the hard drive</u> was defragmented, and <u>vacuuming</u> of the computer insides was done. (Each item in the series has a different grammatical structure.)

Good Writing The technicians **checked** the virus software, **defragmented** the hard drive, and **vacuumed** inside each computer. (verbs in the past tense)

Poor Writing At tomorrow's meeting, our topics will include budget figures, future sales, and <u>we want to select committees</u>. (The underlined item is not the same as the other items in the series.)

Good Writing At tomorrow's meeting, our topics will include **budget figures**, **future sales**, and **committee selection**. (noun phrases)

Create a topic chain

Readers find it easy to follow writing if the sentence topics remain relatively consistent. Study the two passages below to fully understand this technique.

Inconsistent <u>I</u> have lived all my life in Brooklyn, New York. <u>Park Slope</u> is a neighborhood with many ethnic cultures. <u>Harmony</u> exists among the people. Many <u>articles</u> in the press have praised the Slope and its ethnicity.

Consistent Many different **cultures** flourish in Park Slope, Brooklyn, where I live. These different **cultures** exist side by side, and people live in harmony. In fact, the **cultural harmony** has often been praised in the press.

Avoid "which" clauses

Adding "which" clauses to explain your thoughts weakens your sentences.

Instead of . . . The in-service workshop introduced new software, which will reduce our production time.

Say . . . The in-service workshop introduced new, time-saving software.
or . . . The software introduced at the in-service workshop will cut production time in half.

9

DESIGN E-Mails for Clarity

Every e-mail message has one crucial job: to communicate. For that reason, the best messages are crystal clear, letting the reader look straight into the issue with no distractions.

A well-designed e-mail message is organized and easy to read. This chapter will help you design e-mails that give a clear window into your ideas.

Your Goal

Learn about design elements that make e-mails easy to read.

3 Keys to Reader-Friendly E-Mails

1 Use double-spacing between paragraphs.

2 Select a readable, 10-12 point font.

3 Avoid using color, highlighting, italics, or other unusual types of format.

Q Do you find it difficult to read this e-mail?

The following e-mail makes reading difficult. People receive many e-mails and quickly decide which ones to read. Always examine your visual message. Do design elements say "read me"?

An e-mail with ineffective design

New Message

To: Ms. Jamir

Cc:

Subject: Welcome Aboard

Dear Ms. Jamir:

Congratulations on your promotion to our Marketing Department. I have been impressed with your record, and I'm looking forward to working with you. As we discussed, your duties will include the following: overseeing marketing campaigns, coordinating team assignments, analyzing overall efficiency, and providing weekly progress reports. I know that with your help, the Marketing Department will show continued growth and will be able to increase our company's profits. A more detailed explanation of expectations will be provided at our 9:00 meeting tomorrow morning. You will also receive a manager's handbook and an explanation of expanded benefits. I look forward to meeting with you then.

Sincerely,

Lana de la Vega

Marketing Director

Color makes reading difficult.

The font is difficult to read.

Information the reader needs is buried in the paragraph.

Although highlighting can be effective, it might not be readable on the recipient's computer.

FYI Some e-mail programs may or may not be set to display special effects: fonts, color, highlighting. It's always better not to use these.

Q Do you find it easy to read the following e-mail?

You have seen what not to do in an e-mail message. Below is the same message with a professional design that aids the reader.

An e-mail with effective design

New Message

To: (Ms. Jamir)

Cc:

Subject: Welcome Aboard

Dear Ms. Jamir:

Congratulations on your promotion to our Marketing Department. I have been impressed with your record, and I'm looking forward to working with you. As we discussed, your duties will include the following:

- Overseeing marketing campaigns.
- Coordinating team assignments.
- Analyzing overall efficiency.
- Providing weekly progress reports.

I know that with your help, the Marketing Department will show continued growth and will be able to increase our company's profits.

A more detailed explanation of expectations will be provided at our 9:00 meeting tomorrow morning. You will also receive a manager's handbook and an explanation of expanded benefits. I look forward to meeting with you then.

Sincerely,

Lana de la Vega
Marketing Director

A simple black font looks professional.

The numbered list shows what duty is most important.

Space between paragraphs makes the message easy to read.

Q What design works well for a long e-mail?

As always, your goal is to make the message easy to read. Remember to select an appropriate type size and font. In longer e-mails, additional design elements keep your readers focused and your message clear.

Headings If your message has several main points, use headings to help your reader quickly identify the main ideas.

Lists If a main idea has several specific details, you can list them for easy reading. If order is important, use a numbered list. If the order is not important, use bullets to indicate each point. (For more about lists, see page 32.)

Paragraphs Present your information in bite-sized chunks that readers can easily understand. Avoid paragraphs that exceed eight lines of type.

White Space Since white space is part of a design, use margins and other empty space on the screen. For example, use white space to separate paragraphs. The white space should help readers recognize the organization and "lift" ideas off the page. White space also helps prevent eyestrain.

FYI In an ongoing e-mail discussion with one or more persons, each person's text can be a different color. Readers can then tell at a glance who said what in the thread.

Q Should I use graphics?

Graphics give your readers information they can "see." Readers can use this "visual language" to help understand and remember ideas in an e-mail.

The graphic in the message below was attached to the e-mail. We have shown the attachment in miniature. Notice how the writer designed the message to point out relevant data in the graphic.

○ ○ ○   New Message   ⬭

To: (KathyThomas@jaico.com)

Cc:

Subject: Chart for the Upcoming Budget Meeting

Dear Kathy:

After our conversation this morning, I wanted you to see this chart detailing recommended budget allocations for the coming year. Please note that some sections require adjustments to what we had previously thought.

- Personnel expenses (indicated in gray) will be lower than expected due to a number of early retirements.
- That change will be offset by the benefits expense increase (red). Note that these two blocks still demand 33 percent of our operating budget.
- Technology expenditures (aqua) are also higher than expected. This is due to the expansion of our IT department and increased software and hardware requirements.
- To compensate for the technology increase, we have had to trim the office events budget (orange).

The rest of the budget is in line with what we had discussed.

Thanks for your input,

Ralph

Q Should I use attachments?

Sending attachments allows you to e-mail major documents or larger works in their original form and reduces the time spent waiting for a message to open. If you have a large work or a number of graphics to send, it's better to send them as attachments. Remember, the larger the attachment, the longer it takes to download it.

When sending attachments . . .

- Inform your reader that the file is attached.

- Compress large files, if possible, using a compression software program.

- Keep the number of files sent limited to two or three per e-mail.

- Check a file for viruses before forwarding it.

- Check to see that the file is not too large for the receiver's server.

- Save any attachments you wish to keep in a folder on your computer.

- When you must respond to a received file, don't resend the attachment with the reply.

FYI
Consider sending text attachments in Plain Text (ASCII) or Rich Text Format (RTF).

International E-Mail

- Most e-mails use a full-block format. All parts are flush left.

- Some countries format their dates differently than the United States does. Both examples below are used.
  5.March.2006   5/3/2006

- Be clear when referring to hours. A good practice is to use military time to avoid questions regarding a.m. or p.m.
  1200 hours = noon
  1400 hours = 2:00 p.m.

Section 3
Models
and Activities

in this section

10

MODEL **E-Mails**

Have you ever looked at a ship in a bottle? You probably wondered how someone could build such a detailed model inside a piece of glass.

This chapter contains a number of model e-mail messages. They, too, are clear and detailed, accompanied by the graphic organizers that helped their writers build them. Use these models to help you create your own message in a bottle!

Your **Goal**

- Write e-mails that are clear, concise, and focused for your reader.

5 Keys to Effective E-Mails

1 Clarify your thinking with a graphic organizer.

2 Use words that your reader is sure to understand.

3 Choose specific words to create clear images.

4 Write concise, natural-sounding sentences.

5 Create a voice that shows you are a concerned, thoughtful person.

New-Employee Welcome

From:	Julia Westmoreland <jwest@rnkn.com>
To:	Robert Pastorelli <rpastorelli@rankn.com>
Cc:	
Bc:	
Subject:	Rankin Benefits and Policies
Attach:	

PURPOSE
To welcome a new employee and inform him of human resources benefits

AUDIENCE
Robert Pastorelli, Human Resources

CONTEXT
New hire, corporate culture

Dear Robert:

Welcome to Rankin Technologies! I am pleased to hear that you have accepted the Production Manager position. I believe that you will find many opportunities for professional growth with us.

Our Human Resources Department is here to help you grow. Do you have questions about any of the following benefits and policies?
- Profit-sharing plan.
- Medical-plan benefits for you and your family.
- Procedures for submitting dental and optometry receipts.
- Counseling services.
- Continuing-education programs.

If you have questions, please contact me at extension 3925 or by e-mail.

Thanks,

Julia Westmoreland

List
1. Welcome
2. Benefits and Services
   - profit-sharing plan
   - medical benefits
   - insurance procedures
   - counseling services
   - continuing-ed programs
3. Contact information

Professional Thank-You

From: Barbara Talbot <btalbot@hopeserv.org>
To: Donald Keebler <dkeebler@electron.com>
Cc:
Bc:
Subject: Thank You for Your Sound Advice
Attach:

Dear Donald:

On behalf of the entire staff at Hope Services, I want to thank you and your employees at Keebler Electronics for helping us choose a sound system.

We have found that the system meets all our needs. It helps staff in the family room with play-based assessment, and team members tune in to different conversations as if they were in the room themselves. As a result, children who might feel overwhelmed with too many people in the room can relax and play naturally.

In addition, parents also use the sound system to listen in on sessions in the therapy room as therapists model constructive one-on-one communication methods with children.

Thanks again, Donald, for your cooperation and excellent work. I would be happy to recommend your services to anyone needing sound equipment.

Sincerely,

Barbara

PURPOSE
To thank a vendor for providing excellent service

AUDIENCE
Donald Keebler, employees of Keebler Electronics, Hope Services

CONTEXT
Successful business relationship

5 W's and H Chart

Who	What	Where
Keebler Electronics	Sound system Efficient	Family room Therapy room

When	Why	How
During play-based assessments During therapy sessions	Help children relax Model methods for parents	Limits number of people in room More can observe Parents listen

Cover Letter

From:	Melissa St. James <mstjames@dliver.com>
To:	Department Heads <manderson@dliver.com>, <fwashington@dliver.com>
Cc:	<sweis@dliver.com>
Bc:	
Subject:	Checklist Revision
Attach:	New-Employee Orientation Checklist

PURPOSE
To implement a new-employee checklist

AUDIENCE
Department heads and their manager, Human Resources

CONTEXT
Orientation practices, old and new

Good Morning, Everyone:

Human Resources has revised the New-Employee Orientation Checklist (see attachment) to shorten the time that it takes new employees to learn their assignments, company policies, and department procedures.

Use this form for the first 30 days that a new employee works in your department and then return it to Human Resources. Note the following details:
1. The form lists the key topics that need to be covered.
2. The form lists the topics Human Resources will address during orientation and the topics that department heads will need to cover.
3. The last section of the form covers how new employees are reviewed. The review process is broken into four time periods: after day 1, at the end of week 1, at the end of week 2, and after 30 days.

Although the updated checklist will take more time to complete, the additional information will help employees learn their jobs more quickly. Please review the checklist and call me at extension 89 if you have any questions.

Thank you,

Melissa St. James
Human Resources

Thought Map

Key topics

Review process

New-Employee Checklist

Dept. head topics

HR topics

Request Memo

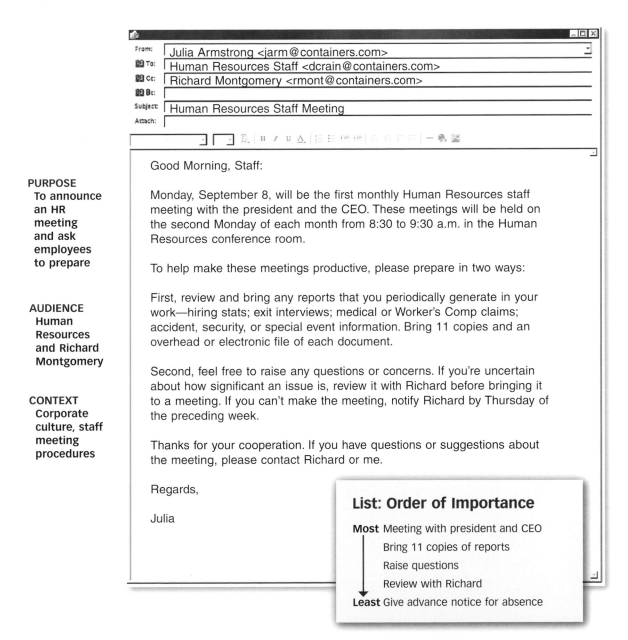

PURPOSE
To announce an HR meeting and ask employees to prepare

AUDIENCE
Human Resources and Richard Montgomery

CONTEXT
Corporate culture, staff meeting procedures

From: Julia Armstrong <jarm@containers.com>
To: Human Resources Staff <dcrain@containers.com>
Cc: Richard Montgomery <rmont@containers.com>
Bc:
Subject: Human Resources Staff Meeting
Attach:

Good Morning, Staff:

Monday, September 8, will be the first monthly Human Resources staff meeting with the president and the CEO. These meetings will be held on the second Monday of each month from 8:30 to 9:30 a.m. in the Human Resources conference room.

To help make these meetings productive, please prepare in two ways:

First, review and bring any reports that you periodically generate in your work—hiring stats; exit interviews; medical or Worker's Comp claims; accident, security, or special event information. Bring 11 copies and an overhead or electronic file of each document.

Second, feel free to raise any questions or concerns. If you're uncertain about how significant an issue is, review it with Richard before bringing it to a meeting. If you can't make the meeting, notify Richard by Thursday of the preceding week.

Thanks for your cooperation. If you have questions or suggestions about the meeting, please contact Richard or me.

Regards,

Julia

List: Order of Importance

Most Meeting with president and CEO
Bring 11 copies of reports
Raise questions
Review with Richard
Least Give advance notice for absence

Request Letter

From: Melissa St. James <mstjames@dliver.com>
To: Robert Taylor<rtaylor@dliver.com>
Cc:
Bc:
Subject: Internship Program for University Students
Attach: Setting Up an Internship, Internship Proposal Form

Dear Robert:

The head of the Graphic Arts Department at Northwestern College has asked us if we would be interested in developing internships for third-year students in the university's four-year graphic arts program.

Internships could be a real win-win proposition. Interns would do the following:
• Allow us an opportunity to work with potential employees.
• Work on tasks that you assign.
• Give you 20 hours of work per week for 15 weeks.
• Get excellent professional experience by working with you.

Please consider working with a student intern during the fall semester. For more details, see the attached guidelines from Northwestern, "Setting Up an Internship." If you are interested, call me before January 29. At that time, you will need to fill out Northwestern's "Internship Proposal Form," also attached.

Thanks for considering this.

Melissa St. James

PURPOSE
To persuade a graphic artist to take an intern

AUDIENCE
Robert Taylor, interns

CONTEXT
Business and college environments

We need to develop internships for third-year students in the graphic arts program.

be potential employees
perform tasks
20 hours/week
15 weeks
get experience

Inverted Pyramid

see attachment
call
Jan. 29

Problem-Solution Memo

From: Jim Musial <jmusial@rnkn.com>
To: Oscar Nunez <onunez@rnkn.com>
Cc:
Bc:
Subject: Software Training for Sales Staff
Attach:

Oscar,

I've reviewed your request to send the sales reps to Cincinnati for software training. I agree that this training would help your staff be more productive.

With your request in mind, I reviewed our training budget to see if we could afford the seminar. A large portion of our budget has already been used to upgrade design software for the engineering staff. In addition, we have some prior commitments for training staff in August. Therefore, there is not enough money available to send all sales reps to Cincinnati.

Perhaps there's another way. If we sent two of your key staff to the seminar, they could then train others in your department. Or we could plan an extensive in-house training session for your entire group.

I'd be happy to explore these or other options with you.

Thanks,

Jim

PURPOSE
To suggest a solution to a problem

AUDIENCE
Oscar Nunez

CONTEXT
Need for training, budget limitations

Problem-Solution T-Bar

Reasons for refusal	Suggestions for training alternatives
Budgetary constraints	Send two to bring back ideas and train others here
Money used to upgrade software	Plan an in-service here for all
Timing is off	

Comparison of Two Bids

From: Barbara Talbot <btalbot@hopeserv.org>
To: Russel Wines <rwines@hopeserv.org>
Cc:
Bc:
Subject: Sound System Bids
Attach:

Dear Russ:

I have reviewed the proposals for a new sound system at Hope Services Child Care Development Center. Two firms, Keebler Electronics and Ascot Sound, submitted bids that met our specifications.

The Keebler bid included the following:
- Sound level adjustment and monitoring for every room.
- Hidden wiring for the entire system.
- A cost of $15,500, with a seven-year service warranty.

The Ascot bid included the following:
- Sound level adjustment and monitoring for every room.
- Wiring is partly hidden.
- A cost of $14,850, with a three-year service warranty.

I recommend that we accept the Keebler bid, which includes totally hidden wiring and an additional four years of warranty.

If you agree, will you please seek approval from the Hope Services Board at the September meeting?

Thanks,

Barb Talbot

PURPOSE
To compare two bids and recommend one

AUDIENCE
Russel Wines, Keebler, Ascot

CONTEXT
Competing companies, bid situation

Venn Diagram

hidden wiring $15,500 seven-year warranty

adj. sound and monitoring

partly hidden wiring $14,850 three-year warranty

Policy-Update Memo

PURPOSE
To outline
a new
orientation
procedure

AUDIENCE
Randall
Poole, new
employees

CONTEXT
Old policies
and new
policies

From: Melissa St. James <mstjames@dliver.com>
To: Randall Poole <rpoole@dliver.com>
Cc:
Bc:
Subject: Update on New-Employee Orientation Process
Attach: Revised Checklist

Good Morning, Randall:

Here's an update on the new-employee orientation procedure:

1. HR will enclose the checklist in each new employee's orientation packet.
2. Rebecca will cover items 1-6 during her new-employee presentation.
3. The employee's supervisor will confirm that the employee understands items 1-6 and then will cover the remaining items.
4. The supervisor will fill out the performance review on the reverse side of the form after day 1, week 1, week 2, and day 30.
5. After the final review, the supervisor and the new employee will sign the form, and the supervisor will return it to Human Resources.

With your approval, we will present this information to supervisors at the next meeting.

Yours,

Melissa St. James

Time Line

First ——— HR gives orientation checklist.

Next ——— Rebecca gives general orientation.

Then ——— Supervisor gives specific orientation.

After ——— Supervisor does periodic performance reviews.

Last ——— Supervisor and employee sign final review.

Suggestion Rejection

From:	Arthur Mellencamp <amellencamp@rnkn.com>
To:	Duane Bolton <dbolton@rnkn.com>
Cc:	Melissa St. James <mstjames@rnkn.com>
Bc:	
Subject:	Offering Telecommuting to Employees
Attach:	

Dear Duane:

Thanks for your suggestion that Rankin create work-at-home possibilities for staff. I've been intrigued with this work concept for some time.

I asked Melissa St. James in Human Resources about the costs and benefits of telecommuting. She said that her department conducted a feasibility study on the idea three years ago and found three major concerns:

- Employees could become isolated.
- Not all tasks could be efficiently performed away from the plant.
- Home offices could prove too costly.

Perhaps the situation has changed since that study. Melissa said that she would be willing to discuss the idea with you.

Please follow up on that offer, Duane. In addition, please continue to submit suggestions for improving operations here at Rankin.

Best regards,

Arthur

List

Telecommuting drawbacks

- **Employee isolation**
- **Tasks not suitable**
- **Costly home offices**

Announcement Memo

From: Brittany Elias <belias@rnkn.com>

To: All Rankin Employees <salsop@rnkn.com>, <babbot@rnkn.com>, . . .

Cc:

Bc:

Subject: New Policy for Air-Travel Arrangements

Attach:

PURPOSE
To announce a new travel policy

AUDIENCE
All Rankin employees

CONTEXT
Old procedures, new procedures

Attention All Employees:

Starting April 1, please make all company-related flight arrangements through the Travel Center. This change will require some adjustments, but it will actually benefit both you and the company.

The business office is implementing the change because the Travel Center is now offering better options for its corporate customers. In checking out the options, we found an attractive reservation and payment plan. Here are some details:

- If you personally book a flight with the Travel Center, you will accumulate bonus miles in your name.
- If the company books the flight, as in the past, the company will receive the bonus miles.
- If we use the Travel Center, the company will have a more efficient way to track travel costs.

You may book your flight by contacting the Travel Center by phone (262-555-8898) or by e-mail (tix@travel.com). Please sign the invoice and forward it to Sherrie Lee.

If you have any questions, please contact me by phone (ext. 9721) or e-mail.

Thanks,

Brittany Elias

Thought Map

bonus miles

Travel Center

DETAILS ——— PROCEDURE ——invoice

tracking costs

Sherrie Lee

Crisis Management Memo

Use a neutral subject line.

From:	Lawrence Durante <ldurante@pmeats.com>
To:	All Staff <pboseman@pmeats.com>, <scaliva@pmeats.com> . . .
Cc:	
Bc:	
Subject:	Recent FDA Plant Inspection Follow-Up
Attach:	

Attention Staff:

I'm writing to share the results of the Monday, July 14, FDA plant inspection.

This is to confirm that the inspectors cited us for three major violations, resulting in a fine of $90,000.

PURPOSE
To inform readers of a crisis-management strategy

We must take immediate steps to protect our customers, our jobs, and our company. To that end, I have done the following:
1. Met with the Executive Committee to review the FDA report and determine the problem areas in our production process.
2. Directed the Production Management Team to review quality-control procedures and conduct two retraining sessions immediately.
3. Appointed a Quality Task Force of both management and production staff to study the production process and make further recommendations.
4. Briefed Sales and Public-Relations staff and directed them to contact customers and media.

AUDIENCE
All employees of a meat-packing plant

CONTEXT
Inspection, factory conditions, public perceptions

If you have any suggestions or questions, please speak to your immediate supervisor or a member of the Quality Task Force.

Sincerely,

Lawrence Durante

Time Line

First ——— **Executives target FDA problems.**

Then ——— **Management implements changes.**

Next ——— **Quality task force monitors improvements.**

Last ——— **Sales and PR handle public issues.**

International Memo

From: Mary Olson <molson@ccw.com>
To: Ursu Longhi <longhi@iikl.com>
Cc:
Bc:
Subject: MW 2.8 Production Book Update
Attach:

Hi, Ursu,

1. MW 2.8 is the updated production book. It reflects the accurate production ratios and image references. It has been posted onto the ftp: Hong Kong.

2. Please provide confirmed costs for tooling, spray mask, styrene set-up costs, product components, and LE kits.

3. Please note: For the US/EU booster case, we no longer require a figure poster.

If you have any questions, let me know.

I would like to receive all costs no later than 2/18. Sooner would be better.

Thanks,

Mary Olson
Project Manager

PURPOSE
To inform a vendor of a production book and request prices

AUDIENCE
Ursu Longhi

CONTEXT
Understood specifications, working relationship

List
1. Tell what was posted to ftp.
2. Ask for costs:
   - Tooling.
   - Spray mask.
   - Styrene set-up.
   - Product components.
   - LE kits.
3. Cancel figure poster.

International Letter

From: Lucille Burton <lburton@hpro.com>

To: Robert Tan <rtan@carco.com.ca>

Cc:

Bc:

Subject: Employee Service Training Modules

Attach:

PURPOSE
To confirm training modules

AUDIENCE
Robert Tan, employees, trainers

CONTEXT
Olympics, hotel sites, KinKaide University

Dear Robert,

As we discussed, KinKaide University will conduct training modules for your employees. The modules will train them to provide services for guests during the Olympics in the following areas:

- Hygiene standards.
- Hotel amenities.
- Restaurant amenities.
- Crowd management.

As we planned, the training will include the following:

- Group lectures.
- Hands-on learning.
- Small-group evaluations with experts.

By next Tuesday you will receive a prospectus and time line for each course.

Thank you for selecting KinKaide.

Lucille Burton

T-Bar

Modules	Training Methods
Hygiene standards	Group lecture
Hotel amenities	Hands-on learning
Restaurant amenities	Small group
Crowd management	

Practice ACTIVITIES

It's time for some activities—time to see whether your e-mail messages will really fly. This chapter includes a variety of short, interesting exercises that develop writing skills. The activities include organizing a message, checking subject-verb agreement, using the right word, and more!

To quickly assess your writing ability, visit our Web site <www.upwritepress.com>. The assessments there will help you pinpoint problem areas and discover just what you need to do to get your ideas off the ground.

Your Goal

● Choose activities to help you write better.

3 Keys to Learning from Activities

1 Choose activities as needed.

2 Read information in the appropriate chapter before doing the activity.

3 Compare your answers with the answer key, pages 111-119.

ACTIVITY 1

<u>Use Clear, Informative Subject Lines</u>

▶ **Before doing this activity, read the information in Chapter 4, page 26.**

The subject line in an e-mail tells your reader what the message is about. It also helps a reader know whether to file or forward the message. For these reasons, subject lines need to be clear, short, and precise.

The 10 subject heads listed below are unclear, uninformative, and sometimes too long. Rewrite them so that the recipient of the e-mail would immediately know the precise subject. Use the questions in parentheses to help you write a clear subject line. (When you have finished, compare your work to the well-written samples on page 111.)

> Unclear Subject line: Attend a Wow Event!
> Clear Subject line: Annual Company Picnic
> Unclear Subject line: Hiring Practices
> Clear Subject line: New Company Hiring Practices

1. Subject line: **The Project** (What project?)

2. Subject line: **A Meeting** (What meeting?)

3. Subject line: **Take It from Me** (What information?)

4. Subject line: **An Invitation** (To what?)

5. Subject line: **A Matter of Great Concern** (What is the matter of great concern?)

6. Subject line: **Thought You'd Like to Hear** (What is the subject?)

7. Subject line: **I'm Waiting for Your Opinion** (An opinion about what?)

8. Subject line: **Things Are Going Well** (What is going well?)

9. Subject line: **That Issue We Discussed** (What issue?)

10. Subject line: **Information You Might Need** (About what?)

Use an Inverted Pyramid

Before doing this activity, read the information in Chapter 4, page 30.

Use the information in the inverted pyramid below to write an e-mail that organizes the ideas clearly. After you have finished, compare your e-mail to the one on page 111.

By-Lo Department Head meeting 9:00 a.m.
Monday to discuss competing with
new Maxi-Mart

Areas to consider:
customer service, stock,
community outreach,
other areas

Motivational
call to
action

ACTIVITY 3

Create a T-Bar

Before doing this activity, read the information in Chapter 4, page 31.

Read the e-mail that follows. Then use the information and details in the e-mail to create a T-bar that shows the organization that the writer used in the e-mail. Compare your T-bar to the one on page 112.

New Message

Send Chat Attach Address Fonts Colors Save As Draft

To: Martha Hidlie

Cc:

Subject: Building Team Skills Workshop

Dear Martha,

I believe the training workshop that I have planned will help the teams in your company work better with each other. Building communication skills should decrease the problems that team members have been bringing to your attention.

The particular skills that I plan to include in the training workshop have been divided into three sessions: "Listening," "Cooperating," and "Responding." Each session will include a 20-minute information period, a 10-minute demonstration, and a 45-minute practice period.

The "Listening" session includes skills to let the speaker know you are listening: make eye contact, nod your head, and remain attentive. The "Cooperating" session includes such skills as using common courtesy; challenging an idea, not a person; and never using put-downs. The "Responding" session includes skills such as thinking before responding, learning how to disagree, and making team decisions. Please advise me if you would like any changes or additions.

Sincerely,

Roberta Wilks

T-Bar

Sessions	Contents of Sessions

ACTIVITY 4

Use a T-Bar to Organize

▶ Before doing this activity, read the information in Chapter 4, page 31.

Study the lists of details in the T-bar below. Then write an e-mail message that is organized around the points listed in the T-bar. Use the e-mail on page 77 as a model. Write the message as the manager of a road construction crew to your boss. (Make up other details as needed.) Then compare your e-mail to the one on page 112.

Address your e-mail to Bill Storm.
Make the subject line read: Problems/Solutions (7/11-7/15).

Problems	Solutions
1. Old sewer lines are crumbling and leaking.	1. Sought bids; BJ Construction is replacing sewer lines.
2. Running behind schedule due to vacations.	2. Asked crew to defer vacations.
3. More breakdowns than usual: truck (clutch).	3. Kept the crew busy: they checked tar sewer grates while waiting for repairs to be made.

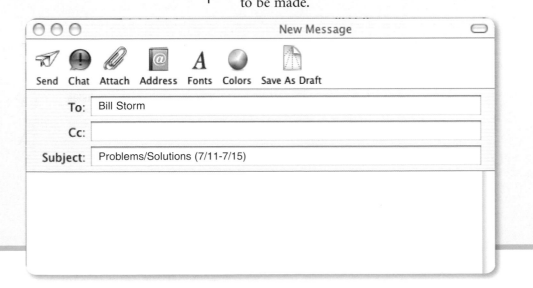

New Message

Send Chat Attach Address Fonts Colors Save As Draft

To: Bill Storm

Cc:

Subject: Problems/Solutions (7/11-7/15)

ACTIVITY 5

Use a Time Line

Before doing this activity, read the information in Chapter 4, page 31.

Use the following time line to write an e-mail that explains the proper procedure for dealing with an injury that results from an on-site accident. Use the time line to organize the information in your e-mail. Add more details if you wish. Compare your e-mail with the one on page 112.

Time Line

When an injury occurs on-site, follow these steps:

First — *Safely* make sure the injured person is out of danger.

Second — Check consciousness and assess the severity of the injury.

- **If the person is conscious and the injury is mild,** apply appropriate first aid, take the person to the health office, and fill out an accident report.

- **If the person is unconscious or the injury is severe,** see below.

Third — Have someone call 911 and stay on line.

Fourth — Check vitals, following the instructions of the 911 operator.

- **If the person is not breathing,** check airway and use a respiration kit to provide artificial respiration (trained personnel only).

- **If the person has no pulse,** use automatic defibrillator (trained personnel only).

- **If the person is not breathing and has no pulse,** perform CPR (trained personnel only).

- **If the person is bleeding profusely,** use gloves, bandages, and elevation to stop bleeding. Avoid contact with bodily fluids.

Fifth — Continue first aid until help arrives.

Last — Fill out an accident report.

ACTIVITY 6

Create a Time Line

► **Before doing this activity, read the information in Chapter 4, page 31.**

Read the following e-mail. Then create the time line that was used to write the e-mail. (When you are finished, compare your work to the time line on page 112.)

```
○ ○ ○                         New Message                         ⬭
```

✈	⊕	📎	@	A	○	📄
Send	Chat	Attach	Address	Fonts	Colors	Save As Draft

To: All Sales Reps

Cc: Juan Galapos

Subject: Sales Process for 665X

Dear Sales Representatives,

At this morning's sales meeting, we created a step-by-step process to meet our sales goal: selling 1,000 model 665X computers. Thank you for offering so many good suggestions. I think we came up with an excellent process.

Here are the steps that we decided to use: (1) Give information orally to the customer and offer a brochure. (2) Invite him or her to our demonstration site. (3) Encourage the customer to experiment with some of the computer's new features. (4) Prepare the paperwork for the purchase. Be certain to quote a price, list the delivery date, and indicate whether or not installation and training are desired. (5) Deliver and possibly install the computer.

Thanks, once again, for your contributions and excitement over this new product.

Sincerely,

Allen Purn

Time Line

First ┤
Then ┤
Next ┤
After ┤
Last ┤

ACTIVITY 7

<u>Write Parallel Lists</u>

▶ **Before doing this activity, read the information in Chapter 4, page 32.**

When composing a list, use parallel construction. Parallel construction means that each item in your list begins the same way. The most common choices are the following:
- An active verb (write).
- An "ing" word (writing).
- The word *to* (to write).

One or two items in each list below do not begin in the same way. Choose the appropriate words that will make each list parallel. (Answers are on page 113.)

1. **Final preparations for Mrs. Forbinski's visit**
   Call the caterer about having low-carb choices
   Check arrival time
   To confirm with airport driver
   Make sure Mrs. Forbinski's name is spelled correctly
   Printing the agenda for her
   Make reservation for dinner

2. **List of Mrs. Forbinski's hobbies**
   Reading books
   Gardening
   To show her dog
   Having guests for dinner
   Supporter for March of Dimes fund-raisers

3. **Today's top priorities**
   To choose a title for e-mail book
   Study bids from printers
   Attending Elmo's retirement party (5:00 p.m. at Kirsten's)
   To have meeting with Marketing (1:00 p.m.)
   To interview three business writers (10:00 a.m., 11:00 a.m., 3:00 p.m.)

Use Adjectives and Adverbs with Care

► **Before doing this activity, read the information in Chapter 6, page 42.**

In business writing, use adverbs when you must tell how, when, in what manner, or where. Use adjectives when you must tell what kind, which one, or how many.

In the e-mail below, cross out the adjectives and adverbs that you believe are unnecessary. Then read the message to see if all the sentences still make sense. When you change a piece of writing, check to see if additional words need to be cut or if punctuation needs to change. When you finish, turn to page 114 to see how one business writer edited the message.

○ ○ ○	New Message	⬭

Send	Chat	Attach	Address	Fonts	Colors	Save As Draft

To: Department Managers

Cc:

Subject: E-Mail Guidelines Review

Dear Department Managers,

Now that we're all familiar with our company's new effective e-mail system, I want to review the e-mail guidelines we wrote back in January. Following these guidelines should be a bit easier now. I would like to begin with a small review of the goodwill messages.

First, we unanimously decided to send goodwill messages to valued customers and suppliers. Who wants to write these important, joyful e-mails? I believe we decided to acknowledge great awards received, community services cheerfully provided, and business milestones successfully achieved.

We need to set up a communication process so the person writing the messages knows when to write a wonderful message. All of us need to continuously contribute to this far-reaching communication process. Who has the best suggestions to accomplish this important task? I know you have given this some intense thought, so let's meet on Monday, Dec. 15, in the new, incredible employee cafeteria at 2:30 p.m. and pool all our significant thoughts. Coffee is on me.

See you soon,

David Yarn

ACTIVITY 9

<u>Choose Specific Verbs and Nouns</u>

▶ Before doing this activity, read the information in Chapter 6, page 43.

Choose what you believe would be the strongest and most precise noun or verb to replace the weak, underlined words in each sentence below. Suggested answers are on page 114.

1. We presented the sales seminar in <u>many cities</u>.
   a. the most beautiful cities   b. Los Angeles, Houston, and Milwaukee
   c. three outstanding markets   d. interesting places

2. <u>Some human beings</u> may face a challenging audience when negotiating with employees.
   a. Managers   b. People   c. Citizens   d. Females

3. Design each visual so that it <u>has</u> one single point.
   a. shows contact with   b. imparts   c. emphasizes   d. lays bare

4. Are we experiencing lengthy delays in shipping <u>to two overseas countries</u>?
   a. internationally   b. outside our country   c. to Sweden and Finland

5. Experienced sales representatives <u>become acquainted with</u> how to answer questions.
   a. know   b. will eventually learn   c. convey   d. gain knowledge of

6. People cannot <u>pick up</u> their communication skills if they continue to write and speak the same way over and over.
   a. grow   b. show off   c. improve   d. make better and better and better

7. Open-ended, sincere questions usually <u>get</u> the best answers.
   a. fish out   b. elicit   c. extract   d. dig up

8. Please take the <u>information</u> to Mr. Weems.
   a. data   b. numbers   c. sales reports   d. reports

9. <u>The business</u> is selling its fleet of cars to interested employees.
   a. The company   b. The group   c. Bran Company   d. The conglomerate

10. Identify the <u>things</u> that cause the situation.
    a. circumstances   b. affairs   c. causes   d. objects

ACTIVITY 10

Use the Right Word

▶ **Before doing this activity, read the information in Chapter 6, page 42.**

The best way to learn these words is to use them in sentences that you write or speak. Below you will find a list of common words that can be easily confused. If you have the book *Write for Business*, you will find these words explained on pages 223-240. If you don't have *Write for Business*, you will need a dictionary.

       see, sea   I *see* the *sea*, and the *sea sees* me.
       two, to, too   I'm going *to* the *two* shoe stores in town. You come, *too*.

Create your own sentences using 10 of the word pairs below. Be sure to use each word correctly. In this way, you create a personal reference that will help you remember the correct usage of these words.

1. already, all ready
2. alright, all right
3. altogether, all together
4. among, between
5. bring, take
6. can, may
7. capital, capitol
8. scent, sent
9. choose, chose
10. clothes, close
11. criteria, criterion
12. envelop, envelope
13. example, sample
14. fair, fare
15. farther, further
16. female, woman
17. fewer, less
18. first, firstly
19. fiscal, physical
20. good, well
21. hear, here
22. heard, herd
23. hole, whole
24. it's, its
25. kind of, sort of
26. later, latter
27. lead, led
28. leave, let
29. like, as
30. man, mankind
31. miner, minor
32. oral, verbal
33. passed, past
34. percent, percentage
35. personal, personnel
36. plain, plane
37. pour, poor
38. principal, principle
39. quit, quite
40. real, really
41. right, write
42. scene, seem
43. seam, seem
44. set, sit
45. some, sum
46. than, then
47. their, there
48. threw, through
49. to, too
50. vary, very

ACTIVITY 11

Avoid Idioms

▶ **Before doing this activity, read the information in Chapter 6, page 44.**

People like to use idioms, but those who have not grown up with these expressions often find them difficult to understand. Study the examples below to see how to avoid idioms when you think your readers may not understand them.

The solution is *as plain as day*.   very clear
The solution is <u>very clear</u>.

Some projects proceed *at a snail's pace*.   very, very slowly
Some projects proceed <u>so slowly</u>.

The project manager has *an axe to grind* with H.R.   disagreement to settle
The project manager has a <u>disagreement to settle</u> with H.R.

Each sentence below contains a common idiom (underlined). Rewrite the sentences without the idioms. See the examples above. (Answers are on page 114.)

1. Some people <u>beat around the bush</u> when delivering bad news.

2. Lets give her <u>the benefit of the doubt</u>.

3. <u>Beyond the shadow of a doubt</u>, that is the lowest bid we can make.

4. I'm sorry I <u>blew my top</u>.

5. Do you have <u>a bone to pick</u> with me?

6. We want to avoid a <u>brain drain</u>.

7. After <u>burning the midnight oil</u>, we reached an agreement.

8. Although your request for more funds may seem like <u>chicken feed</u>, our budget will not allow it.

9. This new supplier doesn't <u>hold a candle to</u> our former supplier.

10. Wouldn't that increase in salary be just <u>a drop in the bucket</u>?

11. We're considering everything <u>from A to Z</u>.

12. We had better <u>get down to business</u>.

ACTIVITY 12

Write Complete Sentences

▶ **Before doing this activity, read the information in Chapter 7, page 48.**

Recognizing and Fixing Fragments

Remember that a sentence fragment is a group of words that lacks a subject, lacks a predicate, or does not create a complete thought. You can fix fragments by providing the part that is lacking, or by connecting the sentence to the word group that comes before or after it.

> **The following paragraphs have 11 sentence fragments. Find each fragment and then suggest a way to fix it. When you have finished, compare your solutions with those on page 115.**

The software development team had a productive meeting with LMQ Studios. Many new ideas. A great deal of positive feedback. The group discussed new products. Including the shell program that Jason devised to allow LMQ employees to automatically populate their spreadsheets. That proposal generated a lot of interest with LMQ Studios. More interest than we've seen from them in about three months.

After the other ideas were presented. The group reviewed the performance of the firewall we provided. LMQ is generally pleased with its operation. Saying that the company can't afford another virus infestation. They indicated that the new security features work well on any browsers they routinely use. Great work on that program.

LMQ Studios also expressed interest. In an update to their human resources software package. They are having difficulty arranging direct deposits. And adjusting for changes in their insurance program. Challenges everywhere. As Jason said, though. Challenges provide opportunity!

ACTIVITY 13

Use Active Voice

▶ Before doing this activity, read the information in Chapter 7, page 48.

Rewrite the following message using active verbs to create active voice. Compare your message with the message on page 115.

> The next meeting of the Kinski, Inc., Board of Directors will be held at the corporate offices in Phoenix on January 12. The newest products will be shown by our creative team. Then the company's plans for future expansion will be presented by CEO Robert Kinski. Afterward, the board members will be taken on a tour of the main facility by Plant Superintendent Jillian Lange, where any questions about operations will be answered. A full itinerary will be sent to you at a later date.

If you have no specific reason for using the passive voice, you should use active voice. However, sometimes the passive voice can soften the blow of bad news.

Rewrite the following message so it is in the passive voice. Compare your sentences with the sentences on page 115.

> We received your recent payment of $37.50 for our Home Workout Center on 3/7/06. Unfortunately, since the Workout Center costs $137.50, we will need another $100. We will hold your check and will immediately send the Workout Center when you send the additional money. Alternatively, we can return your check if that is your wish.

ACTIVITY 14

Divide Long Sentences

▶ **Before doing this activity, read the information in Chapter 7, page 49.**

As you work to edit long sentences, take these points into consideration.
- Do you eliminate words, especially conjunctions such as *and*?
- Do you add words, especially transitions such as *although*?
- Do you eliminate punctuation such as unnecessary commas?
- Do you add punctuation such as periods or question marks?

Divide each of the following long sentences into two (or more) shorter ones. After doing your best, compare your sentences with the sentences on page 115.

1. Despite some recent claims, our products are not harmful to the environment; indeed, they are just the opposite: Our cleaning products are biodegradable, our beauty lotions contain no animal products, and our air fresheners contain no propellants and have no acidic chemical base but are almost completely natural.

2. If a worker is injured and you must treat a bleeding wound, you should immediately take the proper precautions before examining or treating any wound by first putting on protective gloves and goggles (found in the first aid kit located in every department), and once you are protected, use the kit's supplies to clean and cover the wound, and then send the worker to the health office for further treatment; finally, fill out an accident report form as soon as possible after the incident.

3. We need to be aware of safety issues in the production area of the plant, where slick floors could cause workers in the steam room to fall, so we should purchase flooring that will offer better footing for this area and avoid possible injuries.

4. Karen Johnson has reported that our Tulsa plant has some major issues that must be dealt with as soon as possible, so I will be in Tulsa Tuesday and Wednesday of this week although I know there is a crucial project team meeting Thursday morning, and I hope to be back in time, but if I must stay longer, I will call to reschedule the meeting.

ACTIVITY 15

Edit Long Sentences

▶ **Before doing this activity, read the information in Chapter 7, page 49.**

Research shows that the most readable sentences have 10 to 17 words.

| **Rewrite the following passage, dividing the long sentences into shorter ones. When you have finished, compare your changes with the edited passage on page 116.**

Perhaps the most dynamic change in modern automobile manufacturing is the move toward alternative engines, including the most popular, which are hybrid engines that are half-electric, half-gas; solar-powered engines, which are powered by cells charged by the sun; and, perhaps the most economical and promising alternative, the hydrogen-powered engine, which is fueled by the most common element in the world and has no emissions other than water vapor.

Scientists have been working for years to design engines that use alternative power sources, and new research has been accelerated by the rising cost of oil, as well as by the knowledge that there is a limited amount of oil in the world, and they are preparing for the inevitable time when we run out of this fossil fuel.

The idea of alternative power has caught on, and vehicles with hybrid engines—including small cars, trucks, and even SUV's—are growing in popularity. Many models increase fuel efficiency to 60 mpg or more when the engine is powered by both gas and electricity, yet these hybrids sacrifice none of the "extras," including excellent sound systems, luxurious interiors, and improved safety features. Manufacturers are stepping up production since dealers are having trouble keeping hybrid vehicles in stock; some models already have a two-year waiting list, although as technology improves and production increases and more models appear, people will not have to wait years to buy a hybrid vehicle.

ACTIVITY 16

Combine Choppy Sentences

▶ **Before doing this activity, read the information in Chapter 7, page 50.**

Short, choppy sentences can be combined in several ways.

Coordinating conjunctions—*and, but, so, for, or, nor,* and *yet*
Subordinating conjunctions—*before, after, when, because, although, unless,* etc.
A **series** made of words, phrases, or clauses

Remember Commas

Check your sentences for correct use of commas. Follow the rules below.

1. Put a comma before a coordinating conjunction.

We want a new policy, but we must wait for our legal department's input.

2. Put a comma after a subordinate clause.

After our legal department gives us the go-ahead, we will write a new policy.

3. Use a comma between items in a series.

The policy will address using disclaimers, writing international e-mails, and implementing employee e-mail guidelines.

| **Combine each set of choppy sentences below, using the method given in parentheses. When you have finished, compare your sentences with the sentences on page 116.**

1. Our attorney reviewed the case. She fashioned a brief based on her findings. *(subordinating conjunction)*
2. Martha has been awarded the Service Star for this year. She will speak at the Women in Business meeting next Tuesday. *(coordinating conjunction)*
3. Our cleaning company is fast. We are also thorough. Finally, we are affordable. *(series of words)*
4. We dug a trench for the telephone wires. The backhoe overheated. The gears grinded too. *(subordinating conjunction and coordinating conjunction)*
5. We would like to discuss the merger. We hope to hear from you within the week. *(coordinating conjunction)*
6. We will clean your gutters. Then we will power wash the siding. We will also check for insect damage. *(series of phrases)*

ACTIVITY 17

Edit Choppy Sentences

Before doing this activity, read the information in Chapter 7, page 50.

The following paragraph contains too many short, choppy sentences. Rewrite the message, combining sentences where possible. Then compare your paragraph with the one on page 116.

○ ○ ○   New Message   ⬭

✈   ⊕   📎   @   A   ⬤   📄
Send   Chat   Attach   Address   Fonts   Colors   Save As Draft

To: Maintenance Department

Cc:

Subject: Loading Dock Mosquito Problem

Dear Maintenance:

We have a problem on the loading dock. It is the same situation we have every year. It's the mosquito problem. We have pools of water around the loading dock. They appear each year during the rainy season. They are breeding grounds for mosquitoes. The mosquitoes make life miserable for the dock workers. The dock workers must keep the doors open most of the time. That's because we send and receive more shipments during the summer months. The seasonality of our main product creates more demand during the warm months. We make beach and pool toys. This means our workers are bothered by mosquitoes most of the time. Last year we sprayed the area. We could also drain the pools. I have heard about products you can spread on the water to kill the mosquito larvae. Should we try that? Please help with this problem soon. Our workers shouldn't have to worry about mosquito bites.

Regards,

Vana Brown

Fix Run-On Sentences

▶ **Before doing this activity, read the information in Chapter 7, page 51.**

Run-on sentences are two sentences joined incorrectly. You can choose one of three ways to correct a run-on sentence.

1. **Use a period** (or other end punctuation) and a capital letter to make two separate sentences.
2. **Place a semicolon** between the two sentences. Do this only if the two sentences are closely related.
3. **Use a comma and a coordinating conjunction** between the two sentences.

First, find the five run-on sentences in the following paragraph. Then choose the best way to correct each run-on. Use each method at least once. When you have finished, compare the way you fixed each run-on with the way suggested on page 117.

The Bermuda Triangle holds mysteries and, for some people, fear. This triangle, part of the Atlantic Ocean, lies off the southern tip of Florida between Bermuda and Puerto Rico. Many strange things have happened many disappearances have been documented. In 1944, the Cuban ship *Rubicon* was found drifting in the Triangle with no trace of its crew only a dog remained on board. On December 5, 1945, five Navy planes carrying 14 crew members disappeared after they had broadcast confused messages. They were never heard from again. Even Christopher Columbus noticed unusual effects in the Triangle his ship's log mentions "fire in the sky" and "glowing white water." *Apollo* astronauts reported unusual wave activity in the Bermuda Triangle as they passed over it in their spacecraft they had no explanation for the unusual wave activity. How do planes disappear without wreckage how do crews vanish into thin air? Since scientists continue to study the Bermuda Triangle, perhaps one day we'll know the answer.

ACTIVITY 19

Use Transitions and Key Words

▶ **Before doing this activity, read the information in Chapter 7, page 52.**

Remember that transitions and key words link sentences, making an e-mail easy for a reader to follow.

> **Read the e-mail below. Add transitions and key words to link sentences and make the e-mail clear. When you have finished, compare your editing with the edited passage on page 117.**

New Message

Send Chat Attach Address Fonts Colors Save As Draft

To: Thomas Carlisle

Cc:

Subject: Expansion Plans/Environmental Study

Dear Thomas:

It is unfortunate that the environmental study will slow down our expansion plans. I encourage your entire department to work hand in hand with the Department of Natural Resources and other environmental groups. The concerns they raise are issues that confront the entire community.

Rankin Industries has always maintained a community influence. We employ 27 percent of the residents in this town. We sponsor many community events. This will be the 23rd annual egg dyeing event.

I am the third-generation Rankin to lead this company. My great-grandfather would, no doubt, be amazed at the size of the company he founded. His greatest concern was our community presence. His advice to my father, who handed the same advice to me, was this: Hire local people, be good to them, and always be fair. During my father's administration, Rankin Industries went public. He also foresaw the growth of Rankin Industries and purchased the Stoner farm for a future plant. I hope that we will be able to build there. Until we know for certain, I would appreciate our statement continuing to be "I hope we will be able to build our new plant on the Stoner farm." We will refrain from making negative comments about the political and environmental issues.

I appreciate your concern and your interest in the future of Rankin Industries.

Lloyd Rankin
CEO & President

ACTIVITY 20

Edit Commas Correctly

▶ **Before doing this activity, read the information in Chapter 8, page 54.**

Use the three rules listed below to use commas correctly.

1. Use commas to set off introductory words or word groups.

2. Set off nonessential or explanatory elements with a comma.

3. Put a comma between two or more adjectives that equally modify the same noun.

In each of the following sentences, place commas where needed. Some sentences require more than one comma. You will find the correct answers on page 118.

1. After the end of the year we will be instituting a new accounting system.

2. This system which was introduced to you at the last in-service workshop should end confusion regarding reimbursements.

3. Using this easy efficient system can save Marjory hours of wasteful aggravating work.

4. For those who do a lot of company traveling this system should prove practical and easy to use.

5. You will still have to pay attention to expenses especially for overnight traveling.

6. Some expenses including entertainment may be reimbursed if deemed necessary.

7. For example you might need to take a client to dinner.

8. Such a reasonable necessary expense would be reimbursed.

9. Unnecessary extras such as souvenirs or luxury items will not be covered.

10. The new system when used consistently will simplify and expedite reimbursements.

ACTIVITY 21

Use Commas Correctly

▶ **Before doing this activity, read the information in Chapter 8, page 54.**

Use the following rules to use commas correctly.
1. Put a comma after introductory words and word groups.
2. Use commas to set off explanatory information.
3. Put a comma between two words that equally modify a noun.

The following e-mail contains many comma errors. Edit the paragraphs, placing commas where they belong. Turn to page 119 for the answers.

○ ○ ○	New Message	⊖

✈ Send   ❗ Chat   📎 Attach   @ Address   _A_ Fonts   ⬤ Colors   🗎 Save As Draft

To: All Staff

Cc:

Subject: Attend the Annual Holiday Party

Holiday Greetings!

As you know we at King Industries pride ourselves on our warm family atmosphere. We know that everyone from the custodial staff through the Board of Directors has given 100 percent to achieve this year's record business. We appreciate the long hard hours you have given to meet production demand. We also understand the sacrifices made by your families. To that end we wish to invite the entire company including spouses and significant others to a holiday celebration on the evening of December 23.

The party will be a formal dinner complete with dancing at Roberto's-on-Main. Since we want to include the entire family we have arranged for separate appropriate activities for young children to enjoy.

Please RSVP to my assistant Lynnette Bouvier by December 12.

James Michaelson

ACTIVITY 22

Check Subject-Verb Agreement

▶ **Before doing this activity, read the information in Chapter 8, page 56.**

In every sentence, the subject and the verb must both be singular or be plural. Study the chart below to understand singular (one) and plural (more than one).

FYI

Plural subjects end in *s*, but plural verbs do not. It is singular verbs that end in *s*.

Singular Subject	Singular Verb	Plural Subject	Plural Verb
manager	wants	managers	want
My manager wants to give me a raise.		Most managers want to keep the current schedule.	

Choose the verb that makes each sentence correct. (See the answers on page 119.)

1. The problem *(concerns, concern)* all of us.
2. Some problems *(concerns, concern)* only the managers.
3. The summer intern in shipping and receiving *(works, work)* hard.
4. The cafeteria near our offices *(offers, offer)* a low-calorie lunch.
5. All the reports *(is, are)* due tomorrow.
6. One of the reports *(is, are)* about our e-mail policy.
7. Some employees *(retires, retire)* early.
8. If an employee *(retires, retire)* early, benefits are adjusted.
9. The road that leads to the warehouse *(needs, need)* resurfacing.
10. Either the special boxes or the careful handling *(protects, protect)* the contents.
11. When making a presentation, Richie always *(uses, use)* humor.
12. Frank and Janice often *(uses, use)* the overhead projector.

ACTIVITY 23

Check Pronoun-Antecedent Agreement

Before doing this activity, read the information in Chapter 8, page 57.

For each of the following sentences, change any incorrect pronouns so they agree with their antecedents. If a sentence is correct, write "C." Answers are on page 119.

1. The product testers have sent in his final results on our new toothpaste.

2. The product did not test as well as it should have.

3. One out of ten testers found they hated the taste.

4. Three testers developed a rash in their mouths.

5. Five out of ten said the product burned her skin.

6. All found the product turned their teeth blue.

7. The panel agreed that he or she would not purchase the product.

8. Every one of the chemists will have to go back to their drawing board.

9. Harry said that from now on she would test the products before sending it to the outside panel.

10. The head chemist agreed with his idea.

ACTIVITY 24

Use Apostrophes Correctly

▶ **Before doing this activity, read the information in Chapter 8, page 59.**

For each of the sentences below, insert apostrophes where needed. Not all sentences need apostrophes, and some might need more than one apostrophe. You will find the answers on page 119.

1. The Hudson property cleanup is Jane and Tonys project.

2. Im convinced theyll handle it well.

3. Back in 99 we had a tornado touch down nearby.

4. Kates and Lynns cars were both crushed by falling trees.

5. Its lucky they werent in their cars during the storm!

6. There are a number of dentists in the building for a conference.

7. Our manager-in-trainings enthusiasm is contagious.

8. Did you remember its Lucindas birthday?

9. Please check the warehouses back door to see if its locked.

10. Oh, check its first-floor windows, too.

11. The break-in was no ones fault.

12. The company has 12 years experience with security setups.

ACTIVITY 25

Edit Apostrophes Correctly

▶ Before doing this activity, read the information in Chapter 8, page 59.

The following e-mail contains many apostrophe errors. Edit the paragraphs, placing apostrophes where they belong to show possession, to form plurals in special cases, or in place of numbers or letters. You will find the answers on page 119.

	New Message	

Send   Chat   Attach   Address   Fonts   Colors   Save As Draft

To: Class of 1966

Cc:

Subject: Reunion for the Class of 1966

Greetings, Class of 66!

Its time once again for our reunion! This years event will be a whole weekend long, with several great events. This way, you cant give us the excuse that its a bad date because youll have several days to attend! Pick one or all and have a ball! (Thats Freds line.) We dont want to hear any "nos" from anyone.

Fridays dinner is a fish fry at The Two Sisters Pub beginning at 6:00 p.m. Cost is $7 per person. Saturday afternoon bring the whole family to a picnic at Parson Cove. Saturday nights event is the formal dinner at the Reef Inn. That ones $30 per person or $50 per couple. Then on Sunday well all meet at Ken Glasss farm for a family cookout. Bring a dish to pass (see sign-up below). Meat and soda will be provided.

Its going to be a great time. See you there!

Thanks,

Jim and Terese Finn

Answers

Page 20

1. Thank you for the prompt delivery that kept our Doe Plant at full operation.

2. We have already taken steps to correct the problems that yesterday's spot inspection uncovered.

3. Unfortunately, Dan, we can't hire three production workers at this time.

Page 24

Compare the e-mail messages you wrote to the appropriate messages in the chapter.

Page 32

To: All Employees

This is just a reminder to everyone. Last weekend, the coffeepot in one of the departments was left on. The coffee boiled away, ruined the carafe, and could have caused a fire.

If you work over the weekend, please remember these five responsibilities:

- Unplug the coffeepot.
- Shut down your computer.
- Turn off the copier.
- Turn off lights in main area and restrooms.
- Check to see if night phones are on.

Activity 1: Use Clear, Informative Subject Lines—Page 86

Compare the subject lines you wrote to the following samples. Your subject lines may be different; just be sure you included the information that makes your subject lines clear and precise.

1. The Henderson Condominium Project
2. Budget Preparatory Meeting
3. Upcoming In-service Workshops
4. Kickoff for Henderson Project
5. Concern About Office E-Mail Abuse
6. Possible Computer Virus
7. Follow-Up re New Software
8. Update on Jim's Condition
9. Long-Term Sick Leave
10. Sick Day Policy Change

Activity 2: Use an Inverted Pyramid—Page 87

Your message will differ in some ways, but check to be certain you have included the necessary information at the beginning, middle, and end.

To All By-Lo Department Heads:

In order to compete with the new Maxi-Mart being built on this side of town, we have to reexamine our store's image and position in the community. I am asking all department heads to meet Monday at 9:00 a.m. to discuss the situation.

We need to focus on what we can do better than Maxi-Mart. This includes the areas of customer service, stock, and community outreach. Please come to the meeting with suggestions for improvement in all of these areas, along with any other ideas you have for maintaining our place in the community.

By-Lo has always been an important team player in town, and we need to remind the residents that we intend to vigorously court their business. Let's show them what true teamwork can do!

Regards,

Kyle Andrews

Activity 3: Create a T-Bar—Page 88

The T-bar that you created should resemble the one below.

Sessions	Contents of Sessions
1. Listening	Make eye contact Nod your head Remain attentive
2. Cooperating	Use common courtesy Learn how to challenge an idea Avoid put-downs
3. Responding	Think before responding Learn how to disagree Make team decisions

Activity 4: Use a T-Bar to Organize—Page 89

Compare the e-mail you wrote with the one below. When you make the comparison, make certain the information that is boldfaced is in the e-mail you wrote.

I believe we have resolved the **three problems** that arose this week. The first problem involves the **crumbling and leaking sewer lines.** After you informed me that the city agreed to replace these sewer lines, **we put the job out for bids. BJ Construction Company will begin replacing the sewer lines** next Monday.

The second problem is a result of so many workers taking **vacations**. Because of this we are **running behind schedule. I asked the workers to take a later vacation** if possible. Five of them said they could do that. Three others are taking off one week instead of two. This will certainly help.

We have had **more vehicle breakdowns** than usual. This week the **tar truck needed a new clutch**. None of the nearby towns or contractors had a truck we could borrow or rent. The repairs took three hours. **While the crew waited, they checked sewer grates** and removed debris from the sewer grates on Lawson and Kerry Streets.

I will continue to keep you informed. Don't hesitate to call with any questions or comments.

Thanks,

Anne Donatoni

Activity 5: Use a Time Line—Page 90

Compare the e-mail message you wrote with the one below:

To All Employees:

In the event of an on-site accident, follow the procedure presented in detail at yesterday's in-service workshop:

1. Determine if the worker is still in danger. If so, safely remove the person from danger.

2. Check for consciousness and check the severity of the injury. If the person is conscious and the injuries are minor, apply any appropriate first aid, conduct the person to the health office, and fill out an accident report.

3. If the person is unconscious or the injuries are severe, administer immediate first aid and have someone call 911.

4. Follow the operator's instructions, checking to see if the worker is breathing and has a heartbeat.

   • If the worker is not breathing, check for a clear airway and use the artificial respiration kit (trained personnel only).

   • If the worker's heart is not beating, use the automatic defibrillator (trained personnel only).

   • If the worker is not breathing and does not have a heartbeat, perform CPR (trained personnel only).

   • If there is serious bleeding, use gloves, bandages, and elevation to stop the bleeding—making sure not to contact bodily fluids.

5. After emergency crews arrive, all those involved should complete accident reports.

Please follow all steps. Your prompt action could save a life.

Sincerely,

Jeremy Jones
Health Office Coordinator

Activity 6: Create a Time Line—Page 91

The time line that you created should include the following information in the sequence shown.

First	Give information to customer.
Then	Invite to a demonstration.
Next	Encourage experimentation.
After	Prepare paperwork.
Last	Deliver and possibly install computer.

Activity 7: Write Parallel Lists—Page 92

Below are suggested answers. The bold words make the lists parallel.

1. **Confirm** with airport driver
   Print the agenda for her
2. **Showing** her dog
   Supporting March of Dimes fund-raisers
3. **To study** bids from printers
   To attend Elmo's retirement party (5:00 p.m. at Kirsten's)

CHAPTER 5   TRY ITS

Page 34

Compare your e-mail message to the model on page 35.

Page 35

1. You understood the most important points that were presented at the meeting this morning. Thank you for your attention. However, could you suggest ways to make points 5 and 9 more clear? It is, indeed, difficult to understand these complex points.
2. We lost the bid. Let's meet tomorrow at 9:00 a.m. to improve our strategy.
3. Thank you for managing this new project. I realize you encountered some problems last time, so see me whenever you have questions or need input.
4. The above list of improved services will necessitate a small increase in our monthly fee.

Page 39

Compare the e-mails you wrote to the appropriate e-mails in the chapter and the boxed information.

Page 40

1. Compare your e-mail to the model and boxed information on page 39.
2. Compare your e-mail to the model and boxed information on page 38.
3. Compare your e-mail to the model and boxed information on page 40.

CHAPTER 6   TRY ITS

Page 43

Tomorrow, August 17, all supervisors in the Sales Department will meet at 1:30 p.m. to discuss three problems we currently face with the Backes Proposal:

1. Brochure expense.
2. Summer vacations vs. deadline.
3. Presentation attention getter.

Bring your best ideas!

Page 44

1. You can obtain the new software without cost to you.
2. We know that you have requested an extension.
3. Columbus Day will no longer be a paid holiday in our company.
4. This will cause changes in our current production schedule.
5. We will need time to analyze our position, plan strategies, and, then, move forward.
6. We will do whatever is necessary to restructure our department.

CHAPTER 6 — ACTIVITIES

Activity 8: Use Adjectives and Adverbs with Care—Page 93

Below are suggested adjectives and adverbs to delete.

Dear Department Managers,

Now that we're all familiar with our company's new ~~effective~~ e-mail system, I want to review the e-mail guidelines we wrote ~~back~~ in January. Following these guidelines should be ~~a bit~~ easier now. I would like to begin with a ~~small~~ review of the goodwill messages.

First, we ~~unanimously~~ decided to send goodwill messages to ~~valued~~ customers and suppliers. Who wants to write these important~~, joyful~~ e-mails? I believe we decided to acknowledge ~~great~~ awards received, community services ~~cheerfully~~ provided, and business milestones ~~successfully~~ achieved.

We need to set up a communication process so the person writing the messages knows when to write a ~~wonderful~~ message. All of us need to ~~continuously~~ contribute to this ~~far-reaching~~ communication process. Who has ~~the best~~ suggestions to accomplish this ~~important~~ task? I know you have given this some ~~intense~~ thought, so let's meet on Monday, Dec. 15, in the new~~, incredible~~ employee cafeteria at 2:30 p.m. and pool all our ~~significant~~ thoughts. Coffee is on me.

See you soon,

David Yarn

Activity 9: Choose Specific Verbs and Nouns —Page 94

1. b	**5.** a	**8.** c
2. a	**6.** c	**9.** c
3. c	**7.** b	**10**. a
4. c		

Activity 10: Use the Right Word—Page 95

Answers will vary.

Activity 11: Avoid Idioms—Page 96

Compare your sentences to the ones below to see if you have made the idioms understandable to all readers.

1. Some people avoid the main point when delivering bad news.
2. Let's give her a second chance.
3. Without doubt, that is the lowest bid we can make.
4. I'm sorry I got so angry.
5. Do you have a problem to discuss with me?
6. We want to avoid losing valuable employees.
7. After working late into the night, we reached an agreement.
8. Although your request for more funds may seem like a small amount of money, our budget will not allow it.
9. This new supplier isn't as good as our former supplier.
10. Wouldn't that increase in salary be just a small amount?
11. We're considering all possibilities.
12. We had better get to work.

CHAPTER 7 — TRY ITS

Page 49

We shipped your order today, May 3. It should arrive on Monday, May 6. Please let us know that it has arrived safely.

Page 51

I will be happy to start work on August 24, and I'll immediately search for housing. The information about moving costs and the list of real estate agencies has been most helpful. However, could you also send information about area schools?

CHAPTER 7   ACTIVITIES

Activity 12: Write Complete Sentences —Page 97

The following highlighted changes provide possible ways to fix the fragments.

The software development team had a productive meeting with LMQ Studios. The discussion generated many new ideas. LMQ provided a great deal of positive feedback. The group discussed new products, including the shell program that Jason devised to allow LMQ employees to automatically populate their spreadsheets. That proposal generated a lot of interest with LMQ Studios, more interest than we've seen from them in about three months.

After the other ideas were presented, the group reviewed the performance of the firewall we provided. LMQ is generally pleased with its operation, saying that the company can't afford another virus infestation. They indicated that the new security features work well on any browsers they routinely use. We did great work on that program.

LMQ Studios also expressed interest in an update to their human resources software package. They are having difficulty arranging direct deposits and adjusting for changes in their insurance program. There are challenges everywhere. As Jason said, though, challenges provide opportunity!

Activity 13: Use Active Voice—Page 98

Compare your use of active voice with this one.

The Board of Directors will meet on January 12 at the Kinski, Inc., offices in Phoenix. The creative team will show our newest products, and CEO Robert Kinski will present plans for future expansion. Afterward, Plant Superintendent Jillian Lange will take the board members on a tour of the main facility and answer any questions about operations. We will send a full itinerary at a later date.

Compare your use of passive voice with this one.

Your recent payment of $37.50 for our Home Workout Center was received on 3/7/06. Unfortunately, since the Workout Center is priced at $137.50, another $100 will be needed. Your check will be held, and the Workout Center will be shipped immediately when the additional money is received. Alternatively, your check can be returned if that is your wish.

Activity 14: Divide Long Sentences—Page 99

Compare your work with the passages below.

1. Despite some recent claims, our products are not harmful to the environment. Indeed, they are just the opposite. Our cleaning products are biodegradable, our beauty lotions contain no animal products, and our air fresheners contain neither chemical propellants nor acidic bases. All of our products are almost completely natural.

2. If a worker is injured and you must treat a bleeding wound, you should immediately take the proper precautions. Before examining or treating any wound, put on protective gloves and goggles (found in the first aid kit located in every department). Once you are protected, use the kit's supplies to clean and cover the wound. Then send the worker to the health office for further treatment. Finally, fill out an accident report form as soon as possible after the incident.

3. We need to be aware of safety issues in the production area of the plant. Slick floors could cause workers in the steam room to fall. To avoid possible injuries, we should purchase flooring that will offer better footing for this area.

4. Karen Johnson has reported that our Tulsa plant has some major issues that must be dealt with as soon as possible, so I will be in Tulsa Tuesday and Wednesday of this week. I know there is a crucial project team meeting Thursday morning. I hope to be back in time. But if I must stay longer, I will call to reschedule the meeting.

Activity 15: Edit Long Sentences—Page 100

Compare the way you edited the paragraphs with the way they were edited below.

Perhaps the most dynamic shift in modern automobile manufacturing is the move toward alternative engines. The most popular alternative is the hybrid engine, which is half-electric and half-gas. Another alternative is a solar-powered engine, powered by cells charged by the sun. Perhaps the most economical and promising alternative is the hydrogen-powered engine, fueled by the most common element in the world. It has no emissions other than water vapor.

Scientists have been working for years to design engines that use alternative power sources. New research has been accelerated by the rising cost of oil. Scientists are also aware that there is a limited amount of oil in the world. They are preparing for the inevitable time when we run out of this fossil fuel.

The idea of alternative power has caught on. Vehicles with hybrid engines—including small cars, trucks, and even SUV's—are growing in popularity. Many models increase fuel efficiency to 60 mpg or more when the engine is powered by both gas and electricity. These models sacrifice none of the extras. They have excellent sound systems, luxurious interiors, and improved safety features. Manufacturers are stepping up production since dealers are having trouble keeping hybrid vehicles in stock. Some models already have a two-year waiting list. As technology improves, production increases, and more models appear, people will not have to wait years to buy a hybrid vehicle.

Activity 16: Combine Choppy Sentences—Page 101

Below are suggested answers to the activity.

1. After our attorney reviewed the case, she fashioned a brief based on her findings.
2. Martha has been awarded the Service Star for this year, and she will speak at the Women in Business meeting next Tuesday.
3. Our cleaning company is fast, thorough, and affordable.
4. When we dug a trench for the telephone wires, the backhoe overheated, and the gears grinded.
5. We would like to meet to discuss the merger, so we hope to hear from you within the week.
6. We will clean your gutters, power wash the siding, and check for insect damage.

Activity 17: Edit Choppy Sentences—Page 102

Compare your editing with the example below.

Dear Maintenance:

Again, we have our annual mosquito problem on the loading dock. The pools of water that appear each rainy season are breeding grounds for mosquitoes that make life miserable for the dock workers. Since we send and receive more shipments during the summer months, the dock doors are open most of the time. This in turn means our workers are bothered by mosquitoes most of the time. Last year we sprayed the area. We could also drain the pools or spread larvae killer on the water. Please help with this problem soon, so our workers don't have to worry about mosquito bites.

Regards,

Vana Brown

Activity 18: Fix Run-On Sentences—Page 103

Compare your paragraph with the one that follows.

The Bermuda Triangle holds mysteries and, for some people, fear. This triangle, part of the Atlantic Ocean, lies off the southern tip of Florida between Bermuda and Puerto Rico. Many strange things have happened, and many disappearances have been documented. In 1944, the Cuban ship *Rubicon* was found drifting in the Triangle with no trace of its crew. Only a dog remained on board. On December 5, 1945, five Navy planes carrying 14 crew members disappeared after they had broadcast confused messages. They were never heard from again. Even Christopher Columbus noticed unusual effects in the Triangle; his ship's log mentions "fire in the sky" and "glowing white water." *Apollo* astronauts reported unusual wave activity in the Bermuda Triangle as they passed over it in their spacecraft, but they had no explanation for the unusual wave activity. How do planes disappear without wreckage? How do crews vanish into thin air? Since scientists continue to study the Bermuda Triangle, perhaps one day we'll know the answer.

Activity 19: Use Transitions and Key Words —Page 104

Compare your use of transitions and key words with the ones used below.

Dear Thomas:

It is unfortunate that the environmental study will slow down our expansion plans. For this reason, I encourage your entire department to work hand in hand with the Department of Natural Resources and other environmental groups. Most importantly, the concerns they raise are issues that confront the entire community.

Rankin Industries has always maintained a community influence. For example, we employ 27 percent of the residents in this town. We sponsor many community events. In fact, this year will be the 23rd annual egg dyeing event.

As you know, I am the third-generation Rankin to lead this company. My great-grandfather would, no doubt, be amazed at the size of the company he founded. Like us, his greatest concern was our community presence. His advice to my father, who handed the same advice to me, was this: Hire local people, be good to them, and always be fair. During my father's administration, Rankin Industries went public. He also foresaw the growth of Rankin Industries and purchased the Stoner farm for a future plant. I hope that we will be able to build there. Until we know for certain, I would appreciate our statement continuing to be "I hope we will be able to build our new plant on the Stoner farm." Moreover, we will refrain from making negative comments about the political and environmental issues.

I appreciate your concern and your interest in the future of Rankin Industries.

Lloyd Rankin
CEO & President

Page 55

1. Although the front-end loader was adequate when we began, we now need something larger.

2. The shipment was late, and when the materials did arrive, they were broken.

3. Could you, along with two or three workers from your department, attend the seminar?

4. Roy, who is training to be a supervisor, is an asset to our service department.

5. Companies that offer flexible hours usually have happier, more efficient workers.

Page 56

1. Neither the board nor our stockholders want to delay the merger.

2. Ms. Roberts and Mr. Dayton wish to use the mediation system.

3. Either the complainants or the union representative gives the final approval.

4. The committee votes on issues like that one.

5. Our customers and the supplier need our immediate attention.

6. The company's CEO and the union make good decisions.

Page 57

Our visitors from Taiwan enjoyed (1) _their_ tour of the factory. (2) _They_ commented favorably about Mrs. Winston, the guide. It appears that (3) _she_ was thorough and interesting. I would like to recommend that we send Mrs. Winston a note expressing (4) _our_ thanks for (5) _her_ excellent representation of our company.

Page 58

Ms. Prentice of the IT Department has requested that each employee monitor his or her e-mail for spam messages. She further states that there is a computer virus infecting the area. All employees should be aware that their computers are at risk. The antivirus software installed on your computer should be checked. The software can be run by clicking on the icons that appear on the desktop.

Page 60

1. Mr. Kramer's surgeries have paralyzed him.

2. Ms. Johnson discussed living conditions in rural China.

3. The object obstructed his esophagus.

4. Mr. Landis inspired us to work harder.

5. Security investigated the break-in.

6. His answer surprised me.

7. The children performed and entertained us all.

Activity 20: Edit Commas Correctly—Page 105

1. After the end of the year, we will be instituting a new accounting system.

2. This system, which was introduced to you at the last in-service workshop, should end confusion regarding reimbursements.

3. Using this easy, efficient system can save Marjory hours of wasteful, aggravating work.

4. For those who do a lot of company traveling, this system should prove practical and easy to use.

5. You will still have to pay attention to expenses, especially for overnight traveling.

6. Some expenses, including entertainment, may be reimbursed if deemed necessary.

7. For example, you might need to take a client to dinner.

8. Such a reasonable, necessary expense would be reimbursed.

9. Unnecessary extras, such as souvenirs or luxury items, will not be covered.

10. The new system, when used consistently, will simplify and expedite reimbursements.

Activity 21: Use Commas Correctly—Page 106

Compare your placement of commas with this.

Holiday Greetings!

As you know, we at King Industries pride ourselves on our warm family atmosphere. We know that everyone from the custodial staff through the Board of Directors has given 100 percent to achieve this year's record business. We appreciate the long, hard hours you have given to meet production demand. We also understand the sacrifices made by your families. To that end, we wish to invite the entire company, including spouses and significant others, to a holiday celebration on the evening of December 23.

The party will be a formal dinner, complete with dancing, at Roberto's-on-Main. Since we want to include the entire family, we have arranged for separate, appropriate activities for young children to enjoy.

Please RSVP to my assistant, Lynnette Bouvier, by December 12.

James Michaelson

Activity 22: Check Subject-Verb Agreement —Page 107

1. concerns 4. offers 7. retire 10. protects
2. concern 5. are 8. retires 11. uses
3. works 6. is 9. needs 12. use

Activity 23: Check Pronoun-Antecedent Agreement—Page 108

1. The product testers have sent in ~~his~~ *their* final results on our new toothpaste.
2. C
3. One out of ten testers found ~~they~~ *he or she* hated the taste.
4. C
5. Five out of ten said the product burned ~~her~~ *their* skin.
6. C
7. The panel agreed that ~~he or she~~ *they* would not purchase the product.
8. Every one of the chemists will have to go back to ~~their~~ *his or her* drawing board.
9. Harry said that from now on ~~she~~ *he* would test the products before sending ~~it~~ *them* to the outside panel.
10. C

Activity 24: Use Apostrophes Correctly —Page 109

1. The Hudson property cleanup is Jane and Tony's project.
2. I'm convinced they'll handle it well.
3. Back in '99 we had a tornado touch down nearby.
4. Kate's and Lynn's cars were both crushed by falling trees.
5. It's lucky they weren't in their cars during the storm!
6. There are a number of dentists in the building for a conference.
7. Our manager-in-training's enthusiasm is contagious.
8. Did you remember it's Lucinda's birthday?
9. Please check the warehouse's back door to see if it's locked.
10. Oh, check its first-floor windows, too.
11. The break-in was no one's fault.
12. The company has 12 years' experience with security setups.

Activity 25: Edit Apostrophes Correctly —Page 110

Greetings, Class of '66!

It's time once again for our reunion! This year's event will be a whole weekend long, with several great events. This way, you can't give us the excuse that it's a bad date because you'll have several days to attend! Pick one or all and have a ball! (That's Fred's line.) We don't want to hear any "no's" from anyone.

Friday's dinner is a fish fry at The Two Sisters' Pub beginning at 6:00 p.m. Cost is $7 per person. Saturday afternoon bring the whole family to a picnic at Parson Cove. Saturday night's event is the formal dinner at the Reef Inn. That one's $30 per person or $50 per couple. Then on Sunday we'll all meet at Ken Glass's farm for a family cookout. Bring a dish to pass (see sign-up below). Meat and soda will be provided.

It's going to be a great time. See you there!

Jim and Terese Finn

CHAPTER 9

No answer needed.

Index

BUSINESS WRITING AND COMMUNICATING TOOLS THAT REALLY WORK!

Write for Business with Companion CD
A Compact Guide to Writing and Communicating in the Workplace
Verne Meyer, PhD; Pat Sebranek; John Van Rys, PhD

Write for Business, an award-winning business writing and communication resource for professionals in every business field, helps promote effective written and oral communication skills. The easy-to-follow format includes guidelines, models, checklists, and templates to help you save time drafting, revising, and proofreading. Based on the "Seven Traits of Good Writing," *Write for Business* teaches how to write clear and engaging e-mail messages, project reports, presentations, proposals, and more.

(1-932436-00-6) hardcover $29.95*   (1-932436-01-4) spiral $29.95*

emPOWERED Writing Job Aides

Job Aides from UpWrite Press give you the essentials. Four pages of the most useful material, all well organized and easy to follow—just like your writing will be. Carry it wherever you go—in the office, at home, or on a business trip. Don't worry about wearing it out or spilling coffee on it—it's laminated. Job Aides will help you organize your thoughts, overcome "writer's block," and get the words flowing. Plus, we cover the most common pitfalls: word agreement, voice, pronouns, and punctuation; including those tricky possessive "s" situations (Is it *boy's* or *boys'*?). You'll write faster, more accurately, and with more confidence. And the price is as slim as the piece itself, making it a must-have tool for everyone in the organization.

(1-932436-04-9) laminated $6.95*

Effective E-Mail
Practical Strategies for Strengthening Electronic Communication
Verne Meyer, PhD; Pat Sebranek; John Van Rys, PhD

Effective E-Mail Made Easy will help you focus your thoughts and streamline your wording. It covers proven "action" strategies. We'll show you how to write to the particular audience you've chosen—up, down, or across the corporation. We'll go over proper etiquette, how to eliminate e-mail misuse and abuse, and how to manage content and frequency to reduce inbox "gridlock." There's even a practice component, including a way to e-mail us for tips and feedback. In short, it's a system to make e-mail work for you.

(1-932436-03-0) softcover $21.95*

ORDER FROM YOUR LOCAL BOOKSTORE OR CONTACT US AT
UpWrite Press, 35115 W. State Street, Burlington, WI 53105
Toll Free: Call 1-800-261-0637 or visit our Web site at www.upwritepress.com.
*Pricing on listed products is subject to change.